Copyright © 2023 by Madison Schleibaum
All rights reserved. No part of this book may be reproduced in any manner whatsoever without written permission except in the case of brief quotations embodied in critical articles and reviews.

First Printing, 2023

Because the majority of this book was written during times when I truly struggled with my mental health, it is dedicated to those with similar struggles in hopes that they find a way to pull themselves through.

RAINBOW IN MOURNING

Prologue: Introductions

I am a writer. To say that aloud almost feels laughable. I love to write. I was an English major in college and have won awards in writing competitions. I've composed many things from poems to novellas. I even used to while away quiet time in the car in rush-hour traffic by playing little stories in my head but forgot to write them down when I come back to the real world. I suppose I am still a writer at heart but I had once been great. I am now many other things. I am a wife to a military husband. I am a mother to a darling but needy little boy. I am a contributor to the local paper. I am a sister to a disgustingly beautiful and faultless woman. I am daughter-in-law to a horrible wench. I have to be my professional-me at work and my mommy/spouse-me at home. I have to be my bubbly/happy me with friends and family. But I can never just be ME. I have to fit myself into my surroundings like camouflage. I am a chameleon in a land of flamingos. I can see everyone else for exactly what they are from far away but they must never see me.

It's exhausting to have to prepare myself emotionally for the day and the people I have to face. No one wants to see the real me. They want to see the smiling and happy mask I put on in the morning. I was diagnosed with depression and a few other things when I was a teenager and I learned from an early age to suppress what others mistake for sullenness or bitterness at the world. I can't control the pit inside of me that is steadily swallowing me alive. I can't control my desire to sink into the dirt and disappear. I can't control my spontaneous fits of anger and hatred. But I can hide them. I can stifle them. No one has to see them.

When I can sneak a few quiet moments at home, I sit at my computer in solitude and put words to page. It's not much. I can't pull myself to produce the masterpieces that once flowed from my fingertips. But, to put a small piece of my soul onto paper is liberating, though a rare occurrence most days. Only in words can I be me. These times are often at night. My son is dreaming peacefully and my husband is far away for some training or deployment or some other career-related thing. The house is still and silent. My bed is cold and empty. Sleep? I have heard her name before. She is a sweet, teasing mistress. She's a flirt who prefers to stay just out of arm's reach. Nightly she drifts past my eyes and wiggles her delicate fingers- always tempting- but never allowing me to hold her close.

So, I rise in the dead of night. I sit at my desk and try to type but it is often futile and I find myself staring at a blank screen, whiling away the time as the cursor flashes like a ticking clock. However, when I am able to successfully put my mind to prose, I feel better, but I know that none of these creations come close to the written works of genius I used to conceive and I become frustrated. I frequently find myself pocketing a small notebook and pen (should revelation happen to find me), tying my tennis shoes, and leaving my house in silence to roam the flowered hills in peace. Purple salvia, also known as sage violets, grows untamed in our hills. While the fresh air and floral aroma are rejuvenating, my escape is not as enjoyable as it used to be. Newcomers are an invasive species in these hills, much like many of the mammalian residents here. Traditional houses sparsely dot the hills but housing developers seek to destroy this peaceful tranquility by taking advantage of the natural beauty as a selling point. Then they insist on ruining it with cheaply built dwellings crammed on top of one another. With these new residents come their vermin. They bring outdoor cats that hunt the native birds and dogs whose incessant barking keeps away the deer and other non-domestic animals that once helped make this such an enjoyable place to live. For now, they are mostly a problem in the valley near the town at the base of the hills. But, like any swarming animal, they are overtaking the hills quickly.

As I walk upwards and away from the commotion and my responsibilities in search of my muse, I contemplate my life. It's probably not the most mentally healthy thing to do. I think about my amazing husband. He has been nothing but supportive since my career has been in decline. I knew there was something special about him the moment we met. We had mutual acquaintances and would frequently see each other at friendly gatherings when we were in college. One night, at a celebration for a friend who had been invited to study in Greece, things finally came together.

While I have friends, in general, I prefer to stay out of assemblages. Large gatherings are uncomfortable for me but I do my best to appear to have a good time. There's so much pressure to do the right thing and say the right thing. But right for whom? Honesty feels right but I shouldn't tell you not to dress like that because you are shaped like a ripe piece of fruit. Even if I were to word it less brusk, you would still be offended. So, I smile and pretend the cellulite squeezing from the bottom of your shorts isn't causing my stomach to churn. I smile and laugh and act as if I'm there having a good time. You needn't know I find your husband as mentally stimulating as a potato. All you need to know is that I am smiling, enjoying my wine, and engaging in conversation. Of course, I don't seem like at any moment I'm going to bolt for freedom and run screaming into the night.

At the party, I looked around the room and I studied the people there. Our host's girlfriend leaned against the kitchen counter. She was bored. These people were beneath her and she did not like to associate with them any longer than she had to. She pretended to smile, but she clearly didn't care. She repeatedly gazed up to Heaven to ask when this Hell would be over.

In the corner near the door, there was a cute couple quietly flirting. Their affection for one another was palpable though they tried to hide it. Their sideways glances and secret simpers were obvious to anyone who looked their way. He wasn't quite a homely lad, but he was very plain. He had watery blue eyes that were set close to a straight nose. The weakness in his chin was not helped by his flat mouth and large, mushroomed ears. To his contrary, she was lovely. Her copper curls were pulled back loosely and tied with a neat white bow. Those that would not be tamed were tucked carefully behind her ears. Under cerulean eyes, her full pink cheeks pulled her lips into a gentle smile.

I didn't know most of the people who had crammed into that large studio apartment so I stayed close to the friends who had dragged me along. I performed my obligatory smile and laugh as I swirled my wine. That's when I noticed the reflection in the window.

I caught a glimpse of him gazing at me over his shoulder. He was a little disheveled but handsome, nonetheless. I'd recognized him from other gatherings though we had never been formally introduced. Rather than the lustful look I typically received from men, this was one of gentle affection. I subtly turned to look him head-on. His eyes did not wander below my throat and, in fact, averted their gaze when they met my own. Throughout the evening I watched his reflection in the window. He joked and laughed (a sincere and deep sound) with his friends but would look up occasionally to see if I was looking at him too. Once, I thought he had succumbed to cupid's arrow as I saw him rise from his seat and amble towards me. Though he didn't stop for conversation as he passed, he did stumble and lightly brush against me. I felt all of my blood rush to my face and my toes go numb as I saw those crystal blue eyes up close for the first time. He apologized for his merlot-induced inelegance and before I could reply, he hurried away as if afraid I was angry.

When he returned to his friends, I resumed my cautious observation of him. I incorrectly assumed my own friends were too wrapped in gossip to notice I was hardly taking note. They were prattling on about who was trying to seduce our creative writing professor (an attractive man though not my type), who was presumptively going to win a scholarship we had all applied for, and other juicy rumors that I was only half-listening to. I made sure to perform the standard 'Uh-huh. Really?' to demonstrate that I wasn't ENTIRELY ignoring them.

Finally, towards the end of the evening, I heard one of them yell "That's it!"

She grabbed my hand and dragged me over to the couch where he sat with a few friends who had not left yet. "You two have been watching each other all night!" Introductions were made and the rest, as they say, is history.

Just thinking about our meeting always puts a smile on my face. Back then, we were different people. It was easier for me to feel something that resembled happiness instead of always pretending. He was far more affectionate and attentive. I can't say that we became *un*happy but "happy" is far too strong a word.

Then, there is my sister; my wonderful, faultless, beloved, darling, and infallible sister. She is the type of woman who could make Vesta herself jealous. Her beauty is so unparalleled in my family that sometimes I doubt our relation. She's never stressed. She's never sad. The entire atmosphere of a room changes the moment she enters. Her hair is always perfect. Her clothes are always neat. Though her house is always in some sort of disarray, it is an organized chaos. Most importantly, her son is always happy. Whenever I enter their home, there is always the sound of child laughter as if my appearance is the cue for a sound bite. She herself is always fresh from a good night's sleep. A part of me hates her for it. There has been more than one occasion in which my mind's eye saw me bashing in her flawless face or setting fire to her magnificent house. I'm not a bad person but there's only so much perfection a person can stomach.

She was more than happy to marry young. She and her sweetheart had started dating in their teens and married in their early twenties. She had talked about motherhood since we were children. When her son was born, she felt completeness in her life. That kind of true happiness radiates from a person. Her doting husband makes good money in the city on the other side of the valley below so her entire life can focus on her cherished son and home.

My own son is just five months older than hers. While I love him as a mother should, I can never shake that nagging feeling of remorse that bubbles up inside of me from time to time. My house generally looks like the aftermath of a natural disaster. I never sleep. I survive on a diet of whatever he refuses to eat- typically macaroni, peanut butter and jelly, and vegetables. I gave up on painting my face every morning or even brushing my hair every day when he was still an infant. When we have play dates, my sister always comments that I look ragged and offers to take the boys to the park one afternoon so I can have "me" time.

I cannot let her do that. As much as I know I need to focus a little on myself, part of me fears my son will develop a taste for her perfection and no longer love me for the mess of a mother I am. He may live off of fruit loops and chicken fingers and his clothes may not always be clean and I may regret his existence from time to time, but he does love me and I cannot jeopardize that.

She looks at her son with such devotion. I don't know what my face says when I hold my son, but it isn't that. He isn't a bad child but I had given birth to him when I was too young. There was a great deal I had still wanted to do with my life. I had wanted to travel with my military husband and write. I would incorporate the exotic cultures I encountered into my manuscripts and leave a legacy of a well-traveled and happy woman.

Then I got pregnant. I don't want to say accidents happen but...

My family was thrilled, of course, and convinced us that traveling was no life for an infant and that I should stay where they could help me raise him and join my husband later. "It takes a village!" Easy for them to say. They weren't changing their entire life plan to accommodate a child that wasn't even wanted. Unlike my sister, I hadn't had any desire to raise a family. Before I had met my husband, I had planned to move far away and focus on my craft in peace. Then, when I realized that my husband's military career would keep us constantly moving, the plan was altered slightly, but still did not include children. Against my will, we bought a house in the hills near my family and "settled down."

So here I am. The parents who insisted I keep the child so they could help me raise it have moved away. My husband is often sent to other bases across the country for training and other military duties I don't fully understand since he chose to stay stateside for our benefit. My perfect sister is the only friend I have here. While I love my home and my son, this is not the life I want. My life has become akin to a Greek tragedy.

All of this feeds into my depression. It's not something I talk about frequently or dare discuss with my sister. When you talk about it, people either react to you with pity and look at you like you may commit suicide at any moment or with the 'Oh, yeah! Me too!' response of someone who is taking antidepressants with no real mental illness.

I hate when someone says they "feel depressed." Depression isn't something you *feel*; it's as much a part of you as your flesh and skin. You *feel* horribly melancholy or maybe doleful. Depression isn't something that can be fixed with Chinese food, a chick flick, and a pint of cookie dough ice cream. Depressed is physical pain when you get out of bed in the morning. It's practicing smiling in the mirror at work to make sure you've got it right. It isn't just wanting to find a dark place to curl up and cry. It's looking at the knife you are using to cut up your child's sandwich (because he has to have triangles) and knowing that that child is the dominant reason you don't turn that knife on yourself.

A little piece of you genuinely laughs when someone says they've had a bad day. A normal person has a bad day when the barista screws up their mocha-frappe-soy-whatever or their boss was in a bad mood or maybe they got a flat tire. A bad day with depression is coming home and asking your husband to hide the gun you keep for home protection, not from your child, but from you. You aren't sure what you would do with it, but you know it's better kept away from you.

There is medicine. There exists a whole rainbow of tablets and capsules just waiting to magically "fix" your brain. They trick your body into thinking and feeling that everything is going to be okay. But it's just a feeling and depression is a part of you. You know that you are just a few missed tablets away from a full-on emotional apocalypse because there is a difference between 'medicated' and 'cured' and everything those pills have suppressed has been hiding inside of you, just waiting for your serotonin levels to be precisely right for an emotional recreation of Pompeii.

You know it's only a matter of time. Seemingly silly things remind you of that. You know it when you are watching cartoons with your son and taking in the villain laughing/crying in a straight jacket while the camera pans out to slamming asylum doors. You get it. You know exactly how that lunatic feels. You have no real control over what emotion may escape from you at any given second. You want to lash out but feel confined and unable to escape yourself. Maybe a padded room wouldn't be a bad idea. Yes, it would. Being alone with your depression is not a good idea.

Then there's the hero. He overcame childhood trauma of monumental proportions to be an unmedicated, selfless, fully functional member of society and an all-around "good guy" - albeit with a questionable level of sanity. (Who wouldn't question someone in tights and a cape dressed like an animal?) That little boy who lost his parents and grew up to be an idol- he didn't have depression. He felt a level of lost and maybe helplessness that your pills are good for but he didn't have depression. You find him completely unrelatable but take solace in the fact that your son wants to be like him instead of empathizing with the mental patient bad guy.

Then you shake your head and remind yourself that no matter how much you may feel like an emotionally unstable clown in a straight jacket, they are both fictional characters. Real life is much worse.

These are the things I think of on my nightly strolls. Go ahead. Say it. I'm crazy. You would be too if you had to deal with the wench on top of a failing career and being a mother every day.

I loathe my mother-in-law. She's such a prudish old hag. She is always judging me. Nothing is ever good enough. Her son loves me. I bore her a grandson. It isn't enough. After she moved into our house, our peaceful household was completely uprooted. My husband and I fight over silly nonsense because she decides to put a cicada in his ear from time to time and piss it off. She is the root cause of every dispute we have. He doesn't see her evil. He doesn't acknowledge how judgmental she is or that she treats our son differently than the other grandchildren simply because he is mine. If I had my way, she would be in the worst nursing home we could find several states away or preferably somewhere in Siberia.

She had been hospitalized not long after I found out I was pregnant. We thought she had had a stroke. His sister had said "stroke" on the phone so we rushed (I not so fast as my husband) to the hospital. I remember seeing her asleep in the hospital bed. Strokes often leave people mute. I smiled. The doctor came in and informed us that she hadn't had a stroke. She had low sodium levels that resulted in dizziness and she had fallen down the stairs. Damn it. I heard the words "full recovery" and started looking at all of the tubes and wires to which she was connected. I wondered which ones needed to 'accidentally' be unplugged or pinched off to result in her transfer to the morgue. Maybe I could slip something into one of those fluid lines. Then, he said it. She had broken a hip. My husband and his siblings decided that she was no longer safe living on her own. I knew what was coming. I fought her cohabitation with us.

My husband is from a large family. SOMEONE else COULD have taken her. No. They decided to let her choose which of her able children she would prefer to live with. Of course, my husband is her favorite and she chose our home. I think she did it as much out of spite for me as she did out of love for him.

Every day she sits in her chair by the window. Her withered hands pierce a needle through cloth as her eyes pierce my sanity. She complains that the television is too loud or that the radio should be playing shows instead of music like in the "glory days." She nags me to make more of an effort to keep the house clean (though she offers no assistance) or that I should try harder to make myself "appear more presentable."

Every day she sits (when not chivying me) in judgmental silence working on the quilt that doesn't seem to ever get done. Sometimes I wonder how easy it would be to sneak up behind her and run a blade across her wrinkled, sagging neck. No. Her dark eyes, still sharp as if they were the only part of her that didn't age, see everything. It would have to be an accident.

Maybe I could just let her fall on the pavement out front on the way to one of her constant doctor's appointments (that I have to chauffeur her to). No. There is no guarantee she would crack her head. She'd just injure herself further and I'd be further forced into her servitude. How easy is it to asphyxiate someone in their sleep?

She occasionally hums and a slight, but devilish, smile creeps across her lips. I have no doubt she is plotting how to poison that ugly blanket and gift it to me as Medea had done to Glauce. On the table near her chair, she keeps a picture of her late husband. I never met him. He died when my husband was young. I got the feeling from his older siblings that, while she refers to him as her "beloved," their marriage was a tumultuous one. She was bitter that he had to leave town for work, leaving her alone with nine children. I had always assumed that she had soured with age but they impressed upon me that it is just her nature. Understanding this does not make her easier to tolerate. She thrives in a world where she can make others as miserable as she is and my house is that world. My husband, being the youngest and the favorite of her children, is blind to her malicious spells.

So, I escape. I climb into the hills at night. Sometimes I don't remember how far I went or that I even left the house. In the mornings there is usually telltale mud on my tennis shoes. My husband became so concerned with my sour moods and my possible sleepwalking that I had to stop telling him when it happened. He wants me to "seek professional help." I don't need a therapist.

He doesn't understand. He's never felt the need to escape. Sometimes you're just sad. You don't really have a way to explain it to the people who don't understand it. You're just sad. You want to cry but your eyes stay dry. You want to scream but there's nowhere to go to do it. You want to lash out but, in your heart, you're not a violent person. There's just no good way to explain this kind of sad. This kind of sad is frustrating. This kind of sad makes you feel other emotions that there aren't even words to describe. You don't know what to do with yourself. 'Yourself' has become a concept you aren't even sure of anymore. The idea of *who* you are has long been lost on your way to determining *what* you have become. Even the you that is looking back at you in the mirror isn't a you you're sure of. It's not a you that you recognize. There's no other way to describe it. You aren't her anymore. The you you are is a you you don't know.

You know you should feel heartbroken at the loss of yourself. But instead of a heart, you have a big gaping hole in your chest. Try as you might to fill it, instead you just feel even more sad because nothing fills it. This black hole in your chest is sucking you in along with everything you try to fill it with. It's sucking in your friends and family; you are losing them and you know you are. They're slipping through your fingers as they're pulled away from you. You might want to hold on, but part of you just wants to let go for their sake, not just your own. If you let them slip away, they'll be better off without you. They'll be free. They can do what they want when they want and they don't have to worry about you anymore.

Without *them* to worry about you, there's *no one* to worry about you and in essence, you are free too. You are free to continue to be sad, and not feel the need to explain it to anyone. You are free to wander off into the woods and contemplate never coming back. You wouldn't have to worry about that big black hole that's sucking everything in. You wouldn't have to try to fill it because you wouldn't have to try to be happy anymore. You could just be free.

I don't dare say such things aloud. People look at you with concern and compassion when you express deep thought and emotion of anything shy of elation. So, I walk into the hills and through the dark. I breathe deep and feel the rejuvenating effects of the heavily scented flowers and sweet dew. On the right evenings, I used to see my muse and I knew I would be able to write tomorrow.

The Greeks had named her Iris. She was the goddess who traveled on a rainbow, carrying messages from the gods down to the mortals. I was one of those who were privileged enough to receive her divine inspiration.

A rainbow at night is a shepherd's delight. A rainbow in the morning is a shepherd's warning.

I had based my career and, in effect, my

life around this proverb. After having decided to stay home with my son instead of traveling, I was forced to find other inspiration for my craft and I was flourishing. I had once been a great shepherd. My flock would congregate at my book signings and eagerly gobble up my latest and greatest works. I loved my success and when asked what my secret was, I would never tell.

I had gone from an author of culture and refined fiction to one of murder, blood, and gore and I had my muse to thank for it. In the evenings I would look out my window over the violet-covered hills. When the moon was full and bright, through the mist that would settle in, I could sometimes see a multitude of colors arching across the sky. This was my sign. This was my rainbow at night. It was my delight. In a life that I wasn't always sure of, this was my one stay of execution.

In the morning I would comb the papers and news stations looking for it. Some horrific crime had taken place in the valley below and I would use this to inspire my writing. I didn't understand the connection between my muse and manslaughter and I didn't care. She was as true and honest with me as Aletheia. When I would find the article, she had pointed me to, I would research my subjects carefully. I would use my former classmates at the newspaper to get all of the gory details that the editor wouldn't allow to be published. I would delve into the minds of the psychotic and desperate souls. I researched every manner of mental illness and assigned one that was fitting to my subject. I would see through their eyes and write memoirs of their crimes. Though the crimes that inspired my works were real, the stories I created came from pure imagination. I surprised myself with how easily I could write from the mind of a sociopath. My editor insisted that I was gifted. My genius kept us both wallowing in luxury as my art was grabbed up like gold. I was happier then. I didn't feel the need to run to the hills to escape at night unless I was feeling the pressure to put out a new book.

That was then. My funds dried up as months and then more than a year passed without sight of my muse. My husband has to be away for longer and longer periods of time to support us. Every night I hunt in the hills, searching the sky for her as I walk off the day's anxiety and despair. Every Monday morning my editor would call me, begging for me to produce something before we were both ruined. She doesn't call anymore.

I cannot do it. Without my muse, I am nothing. In her honor, I had titled each of my works after one of her hues, but that was not enough to please her. I do not have the power to be inspired on my own anymore. I have tried. I tried to search the papers and the news on TV for something. *Anything.* I even tried to sort through the chaos of the internet. The inspiration just isn't there. So, I press on. I desperately hunt for some revelation. There are the usual gang shootings and robberies gone wrong. But the poetic crimes- crimes of passion and lust- are gone. There is no grace in a drive-by shooting. There is no finesse when a liquor store clerk is stabbed.

I lay amongst the flowers many nights. Exhaustion from my search and feeling forsook by my muse has left me drained and horribly frustrated. My harassing publisher and editor and my dwindling flock haunt me on the rare occasions when I sleep and even more so when I am awake.

I lay in a bed of violets, wondering what has happened to me. I am an artist. I am a shepherd to a flock of avid readers. I was a once literary genius of my time. Fame and fortune were all in the palm of my hand. Why has my muse deserted me and snatched it all away? How could she do this to me? I love her. I am nothing without her.

~ 1 ~

RED

For as long as I can remember, red has always been more than just my favorite color. It is lust, passion, and excitement. It is all things in life that are worth living for culminated into a single arc of light. Red. It consumes me. Red roses, red hate… red blood. No matter how hard I try, I can't stop the cravings for the one thing that truly makes me feel alive. It haunts me in my sleep and in my consciousness. It taunts me but still, I crave it. Red. It cannot be just any red. Never *just* red. It has to be pure, natural red. Not the kind of red you get at the paint store or fabric shop. It must be genuine. The kind of red that is pulled from the living. The kind of red that can run through your fingers. Warm red. The kind of red you can hear coursing through a body with each thump in a beating breast. The kind you can see; the kind you can taste... the kind you can feel. True red.

I can honestly say that I do not know who I was before I discovered my infatuation. I think I was a normal kid. I liked school though I wasn't an exceptional student. My grades were passable but my teachers were all kind to me. They used to whisper amongst themselves and smile sweetly at me when I was in grade school. They often had extra treats hidden just for me or would let me stay late if I didn't want to go home. The summers were a little rough, though. My school-year friends would go away to camp or spend long, lazy days with family in faraway places. I had to stay at home with no one to ride bikes or play ball with. I spent a lot of time playing outside. I would often capture bugs to play with or dig up bunny nests to keep myself entertained. Always hiding from my father. When I wasn't humoring myself in the yard, I was tending to my bruises or comforting my mother while she tended hers. Even from an early age, I knew we needed to look out for each other.

The very moment I discovered my passion for this color swims in my mind almost daily. It was one of those summer days when I had been left alone. When I was around seven years old, I was pacing out in the backyard of our tiny suburban home. We lived in a small town surrounded by hills covered in violets on one side and a great city on the other. It was a less than beautiful day. The sun was hidden behind a smoke-colored blanket from which it peeked out every so often. The air hung heavy with impending rain that threatened with a loud voice in the distance. My father was inside yelling something about the lack of alcohol in the refrigerator. I could hear the screams of my poor mother and the dull strike of fist against flesh.

I had already received my punishment for the hour. When I had come home from pulling weeds at my neighbor's house, my father had already had one too many beers. He told me I was a waste of space and a leech on his hard-earned money. He then proceeded to liberate me of the money I had just brought home and told me it was a small amount but it was about time I started paying him back for everything he had done for me. When I began to cry, he called me weak. He said I was useless and if I was going to cry my whole life, I would never get anywhere. I fought the tears as hard as I could but they continued to flow. That's when he pulled his fist back. Strategically placed bruises, contusions, and other assorted injuries coated only areas of my body that could be hidden by clothing. There were bruises on top of bruises where no one could see.

"You stupid bitch! What the hell have you been doing all day?!" Though the doors and windows of the house were locked tight, my father's voice rang through loud and clear. I heard another sickening smack and I winced as if I could feel my unfortunate mother's pain.

I had realized some time ago that pacing in fresh air helped ease the wrenching discomfort that afflicted my back and butt. Keeping myself moving kept me distracted from the pain and helped me burn off the sadness and anger that were tumbling around inside.

Smack! I heard hand make contact with skin

once again. This time it was followed by sobbing instead of screaming. I heard a door slam and knew that I would not see my mother for the rest of the night. When she knew he wasn't going to stop hitting her, she would go away for a day or two. Sometimes she went to the motel just outside of town. Sometimes she would go further; out past where Main Street ends and becomes a small road that leads up into the hills. I didn't know where she stayed when she went that far. I wished she would take me with her, but I wouldn't ask her to. She was upset with my father and since I was often told that I look just like him, I could only believe that my presence would only upset her more. Why else would she leave a child behind to make his dinner and clean up the resulting inebriated vomit?

I continued to pace in the fresh air. I was going to be alone with him again. How long would it be before he came looking for me? As I walked and wondered where I could hide until my mother returned, I stumbled over a rock that I had not noticed before. I fell to the ground. I stood and I looked at my naked knee. No broken skin; merely more pain and more bruises.

I could hear my father's voice in my mind. He was telling me that I was clumsy and useless. He was saying that it was no wonder he had to do everything for me; I was so inept that I couldn't even walk correctly. I could almost feel the clap of his palm against the back of my skull as he reminded me how stupid I was. I felt a great heat steadily boiling inside of me. Every cell in my body was instantaneously electrified. After a bit of wriggling and prying, I ripped the stone from the ground. It was heavy and pointed. I looked down at my knee, then back to the rock. As if there wasn't enough pain, this stupid thing had to make it worse. I maddened further and screamed as I hurled it across the yard as far as my small arms would allow. I heard a slight shriek and saw a flash of white drop from the old maple tree a few yards away. I stood, breathing heavily, and feeling the rage subside as I stared at it. Curiosity overcame me and I walked up to the injured bird.

The dove's eyes were large, black balls of glass. Its tiny yellow mouth snapped open and shut sharply as it desperately tried to cling to life. Its dainty pallid feathers slowly stained the color of a crimson rose. I could see the beat of his fading heart inside of his breast. It forced more of that beautiful color to pool on the ground around him. It was almost satisfying to see this life struggling. This thing was so weak. So pathetic. I stared back as a realization came to me. I was now in control of his life. I was not as helpless as my father claimed. I saw the stone lying near him. I picked it up slowly. The fallen angel lay there, still gasping for every breath possible. Weak, was I? Useless?

I do not remember what happened in the seconds after picking up the stone, but, in the end, the bird lay perfectly motionless. Its chest no longer rose nor fell; its marble eyes had fogged. In truth, most of it was barely recognizable as a bird. Dainty white feathers were strewn about the ground. More importantly, that beautiful color now coated my arm and the grass. I felt its warmth. I could smell the tangy copper scent. It was the most incredible sensation that had ever come over me.

I went to bed without supper that night as my mother was nowhere to be found and my father had left to continue his intoxication over a game of cards at a friend's house. I didn't care. I wasn't hungry. I was filled with a new, incredible feeling that made all else seem obsolete. I was in an almost euphoric state. My mind was reeling. It was as if I had seen into a whole new world and become a whole new being. I fell asleep with a smile on my face for the first time.

The next day I woke to the shrill cries of my dear mother. I momentarily forgot the pain in my arm as I bolted from my bed and rushed into her room. There lay my father. He was entangled in the linens of the bed. A fabulous crimson tainted the white sheets and his pale face. His arms were spread wide, exposing his breast to the world. There was a hole where his heart would have been had he had one. His eyes were empty. I almost didn't recognize him without the hatred that was generally drawn upon his face.

My mother called the police. Her screams and terror barely phased me as I stood staring at my father. It wasn't long before I could hear sirens pulling up in front of my house. Police officers rushed in followed by paramedics. Pictures were taken and questions were asked. My sobbing mother tried to answer as best she could in between gasps. The officers made notes about what she said and how she behaved. I didn't like the way they looked at her.

My mother and I were taken to the police station in a bright white squad car. I was put in a separate room from her where they had lots of toys to play with but I wasn't very interested. I just wanted to know where my mother was and when I could go home.

They asked me about my bruises and scars. I answered honestly. They asked me about my mother and if I knew what had happened to my 'daddy.' They were nice people. I was bothered by how they treated me like a baby. They even attempted to bribe me into saying bad things about my mother with a candy bar. Needless to say, it didn't work. I could never speak unfavorably of her.

I didn't see my mother for some months after that. I was sent to stay with a family that had twelve other children. I hated it. I hated them. I just wanted to go home. I missed my mother deeply and the other children were mean to me. They made fun of me for being smaller than they were and for being "new to the system."

I didn't know what to do. I lay awake most nights or I cried myself to sleep. I just wanted to go home.

I was finally allowed to see my mother at the hearing. She looked scared and worried. The district attorney tried to accuse her of my father's death. It made my stomach turn to think of that sweet innocent woman being subjected to such accusations that I knew without a doubt were lies. She cried through most of the proceedings. I wanted to go to her but the horrible people at the bench wouldn't let me.

My mother was eventually cleared of any possible charges. The slamming door I had heard that day was the sound of her leaving to go the motel, as usual. There were security cameras there that showed someone who may have been her and they had her signature and receipts. Being that I was a mere innocent schoolboy, it was determined that my father had to have been killed by one of his many enemies. It was not a little-known fact that he was a drunkard who liked to gamble and often became belligerent. I was told that persons unknown had climbed through the open window to exact revenge for some undiscovered crime my father had undoubtedly committed. I didn't ask any questions.

Shortly after my mother was set free and they decided that, without my father, I would be better off in her care than remaining in 'the system' and we were reunited. We went back home and I curled up in my own bed and for the first time in what felt like an eternity, I fell asleep without crying. I never cried for my father. The urge to weep uncontrollably never overcame my body. I never knew why. He was, after all, my father. He had taught me how to throw a ball and fire a slingshot. He had even bought me a BB gun with promises that one day I would be able to fire the real gun he kept in the shoebox in the bottom drawer of the dresser, just to the left of his jeans, and hidden under his old work pants.

Now that I am older, I can barely remember the specifics of my father. In the memories that I can draw of him, he is a faceless apparition. I hear his voice and see his movements, but the eyes are not there. All of my memories of him seem this way, save one. The last time I saw the creature. I remember the empty look of his orb-like eyes. I remember most of all, the beautiful color that spread over him. The marvelous red had coated his face and surrounded his body. This is the most vivid memory I have of my father.

My uncle temporarily became a new father to me. He moved in with my mother and me and took over the man-of-the-house role. He had once been a better man than any there ever was. He taught me the most important life skills a man can pass on. He taught me how to face life with pride. But more importantly, he taught me how to hunt; not only literally but figuratively as well. He taught me that if I truly wanted something from the depths of my being, I should never let anything step in the way. Reaching a goal was a man's reward to himself. He taught me well.

Game hunting was a hobby of his. The first (albeit the only) time he brought me along with him is a day I can never forget. He had told me I was going to become a man. I was ten years old.

He had roused me early and made sure I bathed in unperfumed soap and would not let me wear any deodorant. We could not let the deer smell us, he had said. I was excited. I couldn't have loaded the car any faster. My mother watched warily. She did not approve of exposing me to such things, but my uncle assured her male bonding time was necessary for a boy who had been through my 'trauma.'

The car ride was long. To this day, I'm not sure if we truly drove all morning or if my anticipation only made it seem that way. I watched the trees speed past the window. The leaves had already become a mush of oranges and yellows, and profound explosions of exuberant ruby. They were gorgeous.

I helped my uncle unload the car and we hiked up a hill that suddenly plummeted into a gorge. As we made our way down, I could catch glimpses of a clear, fresh stream. The foliage was lush and held every color that could ever arch across the sky. I could not imagine that a more serene place could exist.

We stopped at a tree quite a way from the stream. My uncle said we would set up here. I was confused. What was so special about this spot? My uncle smiled and pointed up. In the tree was a platform pieced together from old planks with a moldy rope ladder hanging down. He told me to go find fallen branches that still had leaves so we could hide the platform from the deer.

I dove into the task with true enthusiasm and fervor. As I walked, unseen birds sang to me and squirrels played tag in the branches high above my head. This was paradise. I worked hard. I gathered thick branches that had recently fallen and dragged them back to my uncle one by one. When I was finally finished and the platform was carefully hidden, he told me he had a reward for me for all of my hard work. He reached into his gun bag and pulled out a brand-new rifle with a bright red ribbon. I looked up at him in disbelief. He smiled and handed it to me. I gently caressed the sleek metal barrel and the warm wooden butt. It was magnificent. It had a completely different feel than my father's forty-five. He showed me how to slide the bolt and load it. The metallic sounds were cold yet invigorating.

We climbed the rope ladder onto the platform. We sat there for hours in silence. I felt the warmth of the sun wash over me in contrast to the chill in the air as I continued to stroke the firearm. The stream trickled by us with a melodic tone. A feeling of peace swept over me.

The tranquility was abruptly broken by the sound of snapping twigs. A doe swiftly appeared from the brush. She looked around cautiously as if she could sense that something was amiss. She finally bent down to drink from the cool running water.

My uncle motioned for me to lie belly down as he put tight earmuffs on my head. He helped me raise the gun to my shoulder and take aim. I'm still not sure if the pounding I heard was the sound of the deer's heart or my own. In either case, my whole body felt alive. I could see every strand of the animal's sleek brown fur through the scope. Her eyes were deep pools of auburn liquid.

"Squeeze. Don't pull the trigger," my uncle whispered to me.

A deafening eruption filled the air. Then, all

was silent. I could not hear the stream or birds or breeze as I watched her body fall.

My uncle smiled and laughed as he slapped my back and we climbed down. She was motionless except for the sharp rise and fall of her chest as she gasped for air. The eyes were glazed. The wound in her chest was much larger than the one that had been in my father. I took a deep breath. I could smell the tangy copper aroma that flowed from her body onto the ground. That red. There could be no more remarkable color than this. My uncle handed me a knife. He said she wasn't dead yet and we needed to finish her off. He held her muzzle and showed me where to make my cuts. I watched as that beautiful color of life poured from her body and continue across the leaves to where it washed away down the stream. I carefully picked up one of the coated leaves and tucked it safely in my pocket. I had to preserve a piece of that moment... and that color.

We ate fresh venison cooked over an open flame that night. I had helped my uncle hang the body and let the blood drain from incisions made in her throat with his boot knife. We then cut the meat from her bone. I kept staring in satisfaction at the red that had poured from her as we peeled away the skin and sliced away the flesh. I patted my pocket. I had the real prize safely hidden away. A souvenir. I was going to take some of that true red home to be my own.

After my uncle had fallen asleep and the fire had long died away, I looked up at the moon. It was a perfect globe of white light that permeated the whole gorge. I tenderly removed the leaf from my pocket. To my horror, it was no longer that illustrious color. It had turned a putrid shade of brown. I threw it aside in disgust and anger. It occurred to me that the only way to achieve my heart's desire was to pull it from the living. It had to be fresh like my dove and my father had been. My uncle stirred in his sleep. I shook my head and closed my eyes.

The next day we rode back home with cuts of meat packed away in a cooler in the back seat. Upon seeing my mother, I grabbed my new rifle from my lap and ran to her. I beamed with pride as I explained the gift and how I had used it. She looked aghast at my uncle as he carried in the cooler with a smirk across his face.

Later that night, after I was tucked in, I could hear them arguing in the kitchen. I crept down towards the screaming. My mother was angry about the rifle. She said I was too young to have one of my own. My uncle defended his actions. He said it was ridiculous to try so desperately to shelter me from such things, especially since I had already seen my own dead father. She warned him to hold his tongue. He drew back his hand. I shut my eyes as I heard the familiar resonance of skin on skin. My mother held her face in her hands as she cried. My uncle lit a cigarette and walked towards the front door. I saw the reflection of the door open and close in a mirror on the wall. I watched my mother cry. I had seen it many times before.

My uncle did not return.

As I grew older, I became an expert marksman. I hunted quail, fox, deer, and occasionally larger game. My boyhood friends fell away and I found it increasingly difficult to make new ones. In truth, I had no desire for the company of other people. I felt nothing for them. I lived for the hunt. It was all I could do to satisfy my ever-growing lust for the only true red. I had tried working in a slaughterhouse as a teenager. I did not enjoy it. Pigs and cattle were dirty, gross creatures and the methods used to end their lives provided no satisfaction. The best red was pulled from innocence and required more powerful techniques.

Despite the obsession that was growing inside of me, I was what most would call a "normal" adult. I had a nine-to-five as a magazine layout designer. It required minimal face-to-face interaction with my peers and allowed me ample time to daydream while alone in my office. My small suburban town was quiet except for the occasional pet that was found mangled by some unknown beast in the night.

I never married. I never felt the need to. My parents' marriage had been a miserable example of what the future could hold. I felt no passion or connection or anything that I understood was mandated for marriage. The women around me were merely people who served to exist. I took care of my mother as a good son should. Besides, no woman, not even my mother, could ever replace my only true love-that resplendent color red.

*****

It had been quite some time since I had felt so provoked by the melodious color. I was walking through the mall on a stormy evening. I rarely came into the city. The mall had virtually become a ghost town as expendable income became more rare. A few large chain stores still managed to hold their ground but they didn't draw the crowds they once had. I had thought that evening was nothing special. I was buying a gift for my mother. I was walking out of a store after I had bought the perfect bottle of perfume for her Sundays at church. I was feeling quite pleased as I rounded the corner.

As I turned, a young girl walked by. She could not have been but eighteen years old. She looked like most of the other teenage girls at the mall with too much makeup and expensive clothes. But she was special. Her hair, flaming red, reached down to her buttocks. It flowed and waved as she moved, enticing me with every motion.

As she paused to talk to another young girl, I couldn't take my eyes off her. She was beautiful. That red! It was the most heavenly evil I had ever witnessed. As I stared, I knew there must be magnificent red inside of her for there to be this kind of red on the outside. The true red. I could hear it pounding in my ears. It was a drum only I could hear. I could feel it coming, the craving. I could not take my eyes off of this red.

She started to walk away. I could not let this red leave. I had to see more. I followed her out to the parking lot. I watched her brace herself against the angry wind. Her exquisite red locks whipped and flew behind her as she bolted across the wet pavement. She got into her car. I sprinted across the parking lot to my own vehicle. Before I realized it, I was following her out of the city and to the town in the valley where I lived. Throughout the drive, I could hear the red. It was calling to me over the sound of the attacking rain. I had to have it. I never lost sight of her car through the torrents of water pounding my windshield. We headed up towards the hills outside of the town. In the darkness, their normally violet color was nothing but blackness.

We pulled onto a dimly lit street, lined with

little ranch-style homes in one of the newer developments. She pulled into a driveway and got out of her car. I continued on inconspicuously and parked around the corner so my presence would not startle her. I cautiously walked up to the house I had seen her enter. My hand shook as I reached for the welcoming wooden door. I slowly turned the doorknob. Unlocked. My entire body had not felt so alive since I was a child. Every fiber of my being was vibrating as I quietly slipped into the house. I could still hear the red pounding its drum and calling to me. I could hear another sound too. Water. She was taking a shower.

Yes, I thought. Take care of that beautiful red.

I looked around the house and found no other people. I had not thought of what I would do or say had we not been alone. I couldn't think clearly. The call of the red held my focus. I took note of where the doors and windows were should we be abruptly interrupted. I walked into a bedroom with white walls and the brightest pink carpet and matching curtains I had ever seen. This must be your room, my dear. Pictures of teenage girls were plastered all over the walls and mirror over the dresser. Giggles and smiles were spread across their faces. I recognized one recurring face from the mall. I walked up to a large picture above the bed. It was my perfect red-haired maiden and another, older woman with the same gorgeous gift. Mother and daughter.

The water stopped. I stepped into the nearest shadow. She came out. She wore a white robe as she walked into the kitchen; her hair was left hanging in a soggy braid down her back.

I followed. Ever so carefully I followed the red. She sat down at a small wooden table and began to read a book as water was left to boil on the stove. I stepped into the doorway. Her back was to me. She lifted her head. She could sense that I was there. I froze. After a few seconds that seemed like a thousand, her head dropped back down to the book.

The red was calling to me with an even greater force now. I had to see it. I had to have the red. I looked around and saw a knee-height iron candle holder on the floor nearby. I took the candle off and picked up the heavy piece of metal. I calmly walked up behind her. She quickly stood and whirled around. Now was my chance to see the red. I brought the candleholder back and slammed it into her side, careful not to harm the red on her head.

A loud, high-pitched cry erupted from her body. It was the red! It wanted me! I wanted it! I hit her repeatedly. Harder and harder I brought the metal crashing into her body. The point that had held the candle pierced her neck. I could feel the red's warmth as it soaked my clothes and splattered my face. I could see it! The red! That perfect color.

The lifeless body of the picturesque redhaired dove lay before me. The red soaked through her white wings and dripped from her fingertips. I licked a salty sweet drop of it off of my face as I stood and stared at the girl's magnificence. It was everywhere. It was natural red. The kind you can see; the kind you can taste... the kind you can feel. True Red.

~ 2 ~

ORANGE

Isn't it strange how things we see and often pay little attention to can suddenly take on new meaning? A seemingly mundane detail of life can suddenly change your entire reality. It may be a person you see every day; maybe an object you forgot you even had or even a color that suddenly becomes your favorite. You blink and see the world with new eyes. They say a traumatic or inspiring event can trigger such an occurrence. Maybe. Children's laughter is suddenly painful to the father who lost his son. Going out at night is no longer safe to the girl who was raped. The Christmas tree no longer brings joy to the widow without her love to share the holiday with.

I had a simple childhood. My parents, brother, and I lived up in violet-covered hills just outside of the town on the other side of the city. It was a tiny house with no neighbors within earshot. It was a peaceful and happy life of summer days in the woods and fields outside and winters next to the warmth of a roaring fire in the fireplace. It was the kind of picturesque childhood you only see in the movies. My parents were happily married and had built a home of love and understanding. I never fought with my brother. We picked on each other as siblings do but we were each other's best friend. It was a complete and wholesome existence.

Maybe it was this blissful simplicity that instilled me with such compassion. My mother always told me that I had a good heart and I would use that to change the world someday. I was always willing to help those in need whether they knew they needed the help or not. Empathy is a gift that few people are given. I hate to see good people in pain or sadness. I want to embrace them. I want to absorb their troubles and make the world a better place. It's silly, I know, but I would love to live in a world where the wicked are punished and the worthy are rewarded with comfort and happiness. Call it my acknowledged naiveté. Call it my castle in the sky.

Above all, I love children. They are a purity that I often think is too good for this world. What grace there is in innocence. Such freedom from worry and regret is known only by children and sociopaths. I am neither. My mother recognized my good heart, but a good heart does not mean I am not capable of doing bad things in the name of justice. I recognize my lack of innocence. I know I have done wrong. The older I get, the more I worry about my life and the direction it is taking. This fear keeps me grounded. This feeling of self-awareness keeps me alive.

When I was young, I decided to allow my empathy to choose my career path. As a nurse, I wasn't thrilled with my job at the hospital in the city. On my first night, a teenage girl came into the emergency room. She had been bludgeoned in her own home. The bright cherry color of her blood-soaked robe almost matched her hair. There was no way to save her. Her spleen was ruptured and her liver was torn. Eight of her ribs had been fractured beyond repair and one of the fragments had punctured a lobe of her lung. I watched the young girl's parents and little sister hold each other and sob when they heard the news. I had wanted to quit at the end of that shift, but it was good money and I knew the powers that be had put me there for a reason.

Night after night I watched them roll into the emergency room, wheeled from flashing ambulances or speeding cars. Most of them were good people—innocent bystanders who fell victim to happenstance such as elderly who had fallen, car accidents on wet roads, children plying dangerous games while their parents' backs were turned. Others, however, had clearly deserved their suffering. They were obviously criminal through to their very core. Strung out junkies hoping to score a prescription fix, gangsters caught in turf wars, thugs shot by police, and all other manners of bottom dweller would stumble in with broken bones or gunshot and puncture wounds. There were familiar faces of addicts who overdosed time and time again. Their veins were so wrapped in scar tissue from years of abuse that we had to find alternate vessels to place IV catheters. Just as bad were the addicts who would attempt self-harm to be hospitalized in attempt to gain access to pain killers. I hated that I had to try to save them. My compassion did not extend to them. These people deserved to die and I must admit, a little piece of me smiled when they did.

With empathy for the worthy comes loathing for the vile. Drug addicts and gang members are obviously the muck at the bottom of the dumpster of life, but there were some whose wickedness was harder to see. These people had dark, soulless eyes that told me they had wronged someone horribly and gotten away with it. When I saw the villainy in a person as they arrived, I would note which room they were in. If the code alarm alerted the nurses' station there was a problem with that patient, I often took my time coming to their aid. There were plenty of nurses to help them, my assistance was not always necessary and I did not want the sin of preserving the malevolence in this world on my conscience. Some people deserved to die and I did not want to stand in the way of Karma's justice.

I was not always so hardened towards the depraved. At one point in my life, I truly believed that these people could be saved- and SHOULD be saved- both physically and spiritually. How naïve and foolish I had been. I wish I could go back and tell my younger self that not everyone has good inside. Not everyone deserves compassion. Had I understood that when I was younger, I probably would have a completely different life. I would be a completely different person.

Each morning, after my shift, I would go to my lonely little home in the hills. I had bought a house not far from my parents. I suppose I was trying to recapture some of the happiness I had had in my youth when I decided to buy it. I had gone through an ugly divorce at an early age that left me with a void in my heart. One day, while out in my yard, I happened across a kitten hiding in my flowerbed. His little sapphire eyes looked up at me from a mane of ginger fluff. I felt a flood of sympathy for the helpless little creature. I saw the plea for food and shelter in those eyes. I took him in and fed him with the intention of putting him back outside so he could find his way home. Instead, when his belly was full, he curled up in my lap and purred. Fate has a funny way of sending you exactly what you need, even when you don't know you need it. He became the best thing in my life. I now had a reason to get up in the morning. He was playful and energetic. His clownish antics always brought a smile to my face. I kept his picture with me all the time. Somehow, looking at my little companion put my mind at ease. He was a constant reminder that there was still some good left in this world. He showed me that I must have been meant to live; I just didn't know why yet.

My little furred companion was a medicine for an ailment I didn't think could be cured. My break from my husband had fractured my soul to the core. Even though he had been a detestable man whom no one approved of, the ending of our relationship had still destroyed me. I had once truly thought we would be together for eternity. I had believed that his flaws would be easily overcome and my love would help him realize that he could be a better man. One fateful night proved to me just how young and stupid I had been.

We were the perfect match. At least I had thought so. We dated off and on in high school and things went well, for the most part. He would skip classes to hang out in the woods behind the school with his friends. He never invited me because he said he knew I was a bookworm and school came first to me. He would get into his little moods where he would go days without speaking to me, but that was normal. I would see him flirting with other girls in the hall, but he never acted on it and always came back to me. What relationship doesn't have its little problems? As far as I was concerned, we were Lancelot and Guinevere. I knew he was flawed, but I didn't care. I think the fact that my parents disapproved of him helped drive me further into his arms. Hindsight being twenty-twenty, teenage rebellion is not a good reason to be with someone. I thought we were happy more often than we argued and that was good enough for me. We married just two months after our high school graduation.

My parents refused to pay for any part of the wedding. They said I was an adult and if I wanted to move on with my life, I would have to be able to do it with my own money. They said they loved me and that was why they couldn't be a part of a mistake of this magnitude. Still, on the day of my wedding, my father came to me and handed me a small black box. Inside was a necklace with a tiny gold butterfly. The body was made of a pure amber stone. It was this simple gesture- this tiny trinket- that made me feel as if there was hope. I hugged him and the wedding went on as planned.

Looking back on it, I realize how blind I had chosen to be. Sometimes you just know. You don't know what it is or how to describe it; you just know something isn't right. It's more than a gut feeling but less than intuition. It is as if some unseen spirit is whispering in your ear. She is telling you to stand guard. She is telling you this situation is not going to end well. She is telling you this but not using words. Her whispers are more like indecipherable tones that invoke a feeling of apprehension. You want to tell someone what she is saying, but YOU aren't sure what she is saying. The only thing you are sure of is that she wants you to be wary. But what is she warning you about? Nothing has changed. You still get up and face the same melancholy world day after day. You still come home to the same abstracted spouse every night. Your life is a picturesque depiction of monotony. So, what is this non-intuition? What is the spirit crooning in your ear? I carried this feeling with me down the aisle and for the next several years. It was a short-lived union. I had chosen to ignore her, and I would pay dearly for it.

Those first few years were much the same as they had been in high school. He would get angry at me with no explanation and disappear for days. He would drink and get high with his friends. I had no doubt he flirted with other women at the bar. But he came home to me every night. I would lay in our empty bed and gently play with the inscribed locket he had given me on our first anniversary. It was a cheap, gold-plated heart but it reminded me that he loved me.

By happiest accident, I became pregnant but eventually found myself on prescribed bed rest. I was only seven months into my pregnancy, but my doctor feared for the baby's health. I was a full-time college student and a full-time intern at the hospital, on-call for the maternity ward twenty-four hours a day. I was going to specialize in obstetrics. I loved babies. My husband and I were barely adults ourselves. I was only twenty-one years old and he was twenty-two. Being young and ignorant, life was what I believed to be bliss.

I lay on the couch alone in our cluttered little maisonette in the city. I hadn't wanted to live here. It was far away from my parents and the flowered hills I had grown up in, but we had to go where there was work for both of us and I needed to be closer to school.

The couch was a broken-down mess, as were the vast majority of our belongings. Most of it was mismatched bits we had amassed from hand-me-downs and yard sales. He promised me one day we would have pretty new things to fill the beautiful house we would own. I never expected any of this, but I didn't care. It was wonderful to dream of our beautiful future family and that our children would want for nothing.

As I sat sunken into the couch watching a blur on our old tube television, the door swung open violently and he marched in. He reeked of cigarettes, beer, and cheap booze. His eyes were drooping and his face was red. Unfortunately, I had grown accustomed to this. He was a mean drunk and often went out on benders with his buddies from work.

Many nights they would be in my living room with a deck of cards and cases of cheap beer. They were always drunk. Sometimes they would be drinking until the early morning hours. Their boisterous voices would rise up the staircase and through the bedroom door. I would lay in bed alone, waiting for him to trudge to bed, maybe kiss me good night, and pass out beside me. I would remind myself to be grateful that it was my bed he came home to every night.

This fateful night, I was resting on the couch on the main level of our home. The little life inside of me had not been ready for bed and had been doing summersaults for the last hour.

I tried to calm her with tea and a good book so I hopefully could get some sleep. If I had only known what was coming. If I had known HE was coming...

He had been out with friends again. I knew he would be drinking but I was unsure of the degree. When he arrived home, he slammed the door behind him. He demanded sex but I refused. He could be a violent drunk but I had become skilled at diffusing him. I protested not only on my behalf but for the safety of the life inside me. He grew red with fury at my rejection. I refused again as I struggled to my feet. I told him I was going to bed and that he could join me- for sleep only- when he had calmed down. He grabbed me by my ponytail and dragged me up the stairs into the bedroom. He threw me on the bed. I bounced off and hit my head on the corner of the nightstand.

When I awoke, it was dark all around me. My eyes slowly adjusted to allow in the minute light from the plug-in nightlight. There was a black stain on the sheets and floor. My head and body throbbed. Everything was still blurry but

I managed to stumble to the telephone. I dialed 911 before falling unconscious again.

When I awoke again, I was in the emergency room. Everything was foggy. My head was throbbing and it was difficult to focus. I could see the EKG blip with my heartbeat, a little light on the monitor showed green. I tried to move, but it was painful and I had an I.V. catheter in the crook of each elbow. I followed the tube from my right arm up to a bag of fluids on a pump. Lactated ringer's solution to keep me hydrated. I followed the tube from my left arm. It led to a nearly empty double unit bag of O-Negative. I looked down at my belly. Where it had once bulged from the new life growing inside, it now lay flat. I began to sob uncontrollably and screamed for help. A nurse came running to my aid. She held my arms down as I screamed and fought her. She tried to comfort me as she told me what had happened.

The EMT had found me in my apartment alone. My husband had raped and sodomized me and the violent manner had killed my baby. My apartment was a crime scene and my husband was a fugitive.

I was questioned by a barrage of doctors, nurses, and detectives. The more questions they asked, the more my emotions changed. When they finally told me that it would be unlikely that I would ever be able to conceive again, my heart vaulted from depression to anger to hatred then numbness. It was too surreal. I mostly cried myself to sleep between interrogations, hoping that when I woke it would all have turned out to be a horrible nightmare. Of course, I was not so fortunate. My family came to console me, but I did not want their pity.

After the trial and inevitable divorce, I moved back to my little town in the violet hills. My parents were thrilled. I hated it. I hated bringing my despair to a place that had once filled me with such happiness. I was surrounded by people and places with such fond memories but these things no longer brought me warmth or joy.

Most days I just felt broken. There are no other words to describe it. I wasn't whole. I wasn't me. I could feel pieces of me scattered around here and there. Sometimes a conversation would make me smile. Sometimes I'd see a picture and remember something happy but not actually feel it. Sometimes I would have a glimpse of the whole me. These pieces were spread far and wide. I would try to pick them up and attempt to fit them back together; to build myself back bit-by-bit but it never lasted. I would fall apart again. I would fall back into self-destructive tendencies. I would distance myself from friends and family. I tried to bury myself in work- that comfortable cocoon that blocks the realities of life. It gave me something to focus on and control. It wasn't always my career. Many times, it would be household chores or a minor detail that I had built into a crisis that needed my immediate attention. Nonetheless, the slight comfort in my solitude and perceived control was there.

My friends and family tried to reach out to me. They wanted to "fix" me or just wanted me to get over it. It wasn't that simple. Did they think I enjoyed feeling myself decay? Many times, I couldn't help but think that they didn't want me to get better for me; they wanted it for themselves. They didn't know how to handle all of my pieces being strewn about and because they didn't know how to glue them back together, they were uncomfortable. They wanted me "better" so they could return to their own comfort zone. They were frustrated with me but I couldn't help it. They were angry with me and I didn't know what to say. I didn't want them to pick up my pieces. I didn't want them to make me "better." I wanted them to be there for me but not try to "fix" me. I couldn't be fixed. Their frustration with that fact only made me feel worse. They didn't realize that once you break a plate, you can fit the pieces back together but it's still fragile and you can still see the cracks.

Every night I would lay my head on a pillow and lie awake feeling guilty. I felt selfish for isolating myself. I felt remorse for the pain I was causing the people around me. I didn't want to be like that. I promised I would try to be the old me tomorrow. If I was fortunate enough for sleep to come, I would wake up in the morning still just as broken. I would remember my promise and I would try but I knew in my heart that it was a pointless effort. The pieces weren't all there. I could find a few and I could build something that kind of resembled the old me, but that was a tower that toppled quickly. When things started to come crashing down, I retreated. I would go back to my cocoon, back to my safe little hiding place. I would peek out and see one of my pieces lying just within arm's length, but it was just too risky to reach for it.

So, this is where I stayed. I was trapped in my cocoon. I knew my pieces were out there and I knew there was a way to make them fit back together- not fixed- but stable. After many failed attempts at finding them all, it got harder and harder to leave my cocoon. It got harder and harder to search for them all. Going to sleep was difficult. Waking up was tiring. Leaving my cocoon felt almost impossible so I wondered why I should try. But then I would see the people I loved and I wanted to try to be the old me for them. So, I would lay my head on a pillow at night and promise to try again tomorrow.

My parents did the best they could to take care of me and reassured me that since my husband had been brought to justice I would move on with my life. My brother always tried to cheer me up in a way only a brother could. He would tell me to get a grip and quit whining.

To just do something. Just because I couldn't have what I wanted that didn't mean I should complain about it. I'd worked hard to come the few steps that I had. I needed to keep fighting and eventually, I'd get there. Life was not necessarily a waste of time. I was almost to the goal line. A few more touchdowns and I'd win. Despite their best efforts, the numbness and sadness continued. I stayed in bed all day and night. How could this have happened to me? My baby, my love, and my life- they were all gone. I didn't want to live, but I did.

When my wrists had healed and I was allowed to leave the hospital once again, I decided to take my brother's advice and try to get a grip on my life, I attempted to return to the maternity ward. The first baby I helped would be the last. I couldn't bear the way the mother looked at the swaddled bundle in her arms. A secret smile crept through her eyes. She was in love. This love was one that could never be conquered or tamed or even matched. That child would be her whole world. That feeling had been stolen from me.

I decided that I could not continue to work

there. The loss of my own child was too much and I could not bear to see all of the happy mothers parading in front of me daily. I had befriended the nurse who had come to comfort me in the hospital and she convinced me to work in the ER after I had graduated.

Every day was a struggle. I wanted my old life back. I wanted to be happy again. It was hard to imagine that such things could ever happen to me. One day, one of the orderlies nervously tapped me on the shoulder. He scratched behind his head as he asked me to join him for lunch. I smiled. I had no interest in this man. He wasn't tall, dark, or handsome. He was rather plain and nothing special. Still, something inside me bubbled up and I agreed.

The next day we went to a friendly little bistro on the edge of the river. He asked me to tell him about myself. I did. He told me he couldn't believe men like my ex were still alive. He said I must have been a strong woman to have endured such a rough love life. I pointed out that I was still single so obviously something had gone wrong. He was mortified by how negative my view seemed to be. I told him negativity was a realistic look at life as long as there is enough happiness to keep you sane. He was less than amused. Lunch ended early.

I came home disheartened. I flopped on the couch. My cat looked at me. I felt guilty. I knew part of me said what I had at lunch to drive this man off. Yet, there I was, feeling lonely and sorry for myself. That night, I looked in the mirror. I barely recognized the woman who looked back at me. Her raven hair flowed down over her bare back. It depicted a scene of a dreary night, accompanied by her starless eyes. She was a sad and shattered shell of a woman that had once held a vibrant soul.

As the years rolled on after the divorce, isolation weighed on my heart and I asked myself every morning why I bothered to get out of bed. People don't understand how much physical pain accompanies a broken heart. Have you ever been in that not-quite suicidal place? That place where you're not sure if you should be alive or not so you contemplate going to bed with a knife. If you roll over on it and fatally wound yourself in your sleep, it's because the powers that be wanted you to die. If you wake up the next morning unharmed, then you must be meant to live. Your logical brain tells you not to try to kill yourself again but if you leave it up to fate, it's something entirely different.

After a suicide attempt, everyone has an opinion. Your friends tell you how selfish you are; they ask why you didn't think about how hurting yourself would hurt them. Your doctor says your brain is broken and you need drugs and therapy to fix it. Your counselor tells you God wasn't ready for you while simultaneously telling you suicide is a one-way ticket to Hell. Your family tells you you're young and you have too much to live for.

So many people have input and opinions on the value of your life and theories about why you did it. It's always hardest when people say it was for attention. If you succeeded, you wouldn't exactly be reveling in that attention. If you wanted attention, you would have told someone of your intentions first. You would have used a method easier to survive. But you didn't. You posted to social media that your day was great and you told your friends at work you'll see them tomorrow. You went home to your empty house and felt the emptiness move from around you to the inside of you.

The logical part of your brain is still functioning. You have friends, family, a home, and a job. You have everything that makes life worth living. But that part of your brain isn't speaking loudly enough. That voice can't drown out the overwhelming feeling that none of it matters and it would be better if you were just not in this world. You don't know why you feel this way but you can't ignore it.

One night, while at work, a beautiful pregnant woman in a purple dress came in. At first, it seemed like a normal maternity case and we prepared to send her on to the appropriate ward. Her husband kept insisting that she was not well but we assured him that the maternity nurses would know what to do for her. On the way to the elevator, her eyes rolled back and she slumped in the wheelchair like a corpse. The orderly immediately yelled for help and wheeled her into the nearest open room.

A surgeon scrubbed in and opened her abdomen to try and get the baby out. I had never seen blood pour from an incision so profusely.

It flowed from her body faster than we could suction it out of the doctor's way. We ran lines for transfusion bags, but the blood seemed to go in her arm and out through her abdomen. We worked for hours trying to help her. In the end, our efforts were all but futile. The little girl lived. Her mother did not.

We pulled the sheet over her porcelain face and I reached for the heart monitor. The orange light blinked and a soft, half-buzzing, half-siren sound accompanied it, signaling that the patient had flat-lined. I watched it for a moment. I had never really paid this close attention to it before. My mentor and good friend had once told me that "green was good, yellow was yelling, and orange meant it was over." My heart sank and I turned off the monitor and watched the orange light fade to off.

I watched the doctor tell the woman's husband her fate. I could pinpoint the precise instant his heart broke. He fell to the floor wailing in grief. I put my back against the wall and sighed. I hated when things like this happened. This woman was clearly loved and she couldn't be saved. I was glad we had tried though our efforts had been in vain. Unlike so many others, she was one of the innocents. She deserved to be saved.

I pulled the picture of my cat from my back pocket. There was still something good in this world. I looked across the hall and saw the man we had triaged earlier that evening. I was strangely drawn into his room.

He lay unconscious. He had tried to rape a woman in the night but she had hit him in the temple with a flashlight. Had she hit him harder, she most likely could have killed him. But, alas, evil lives on. I looked at his heart monitor. Green light.

That night I went home and showered for almost an hour. I scrubbed my flesh in the steaming water until I turned bright red. It was as if I was trying to literally wash the sadness from my body. When I was satisfied, I wrapped myself in a robe and strode into the living room.

My cat was chewing on something. He was good at finding mischief. I knelt down and took it away from him. Where had he gotten this? It was the locket my ex-husband had given me on our first anniversary. I opened it. *You are my sanity.* The inscription brought tears to my eyes. It pained me to think that I had once been stupid enough to believe those words. I thought back to the last night I had seen him and how he had destroyed me. I took the necklace and threw it down the garbage disposal. I was a changed woman because of that man. I did not need reminders of him in my life.

I barely slept that night. That little locket had been a key that unlocked my nightmares again. I saw my husband drunk and angry standing over me. I watched my round belly deflate like a balloon as he laughed. I was running in the darkness. I could hear a baby crying but I was unable to find it. I was unable to help it. I hadn't had dreams like those in quite some time. I woke in tears and vomited. I sobbed and held my little orange companion close, allowing his purr to calm me as I felt my heartbeat slow to normal and my eyes started to dry.

The next night, I clocked in and immediately went to the room where we had lost the pregnant woman. Part of me hoped to see her laying there, the light on the monitor shining green. I knew it couldn't be possible, but I wanted it to be. I thought of her husband. He as so loving, unlike mine. What if I had died that night and our baby had lived? What would he have done to her? Would she have survived without the protection and guidance of a mother? Would he have even kept her? Given her away? Killed her anyway? I didn't know. It didn't matter. I had lived and my baby had not. In a few years, my husband would be allowed to return to society and live as if nothing ever happened.

I looked down the hall into the other room. As I walked in, the rapist lay there still. His monitor light was green as he slumbered soundly. I felt as if there was a great chasm where my heart should be. I looked at the scars on my wrists. I looked back at the bed and saw my ex-husband lying there. A rapist. A destroyer of lives. Why should someone like this live? It wasn't right!

I took the picture of my cat out of the pocket of my scrubs. There was still a small shred of good in this world. I touched his orange fur as if I could feel its softness. I looked back to the bastard that lay before me, then up to his monitor. Maybe karma needed a little help.

I pulled an empty syringe out of a drawer.

I pulled the plunger back and watched it fill with air. I injected the normally harmless gas into his IV line. I watched as the pump forced it down the tube and into his arm. Seconds later I watched his face contort with pain. He began to gasp heavily. I disconnected the alarm that would have called the nurses to his aid. I watched him writhe and the light on his monitor turned from green, to yellow, and finally to orange. He lay still. His skin turned to a pale gray.

As I left the room, I glanced over my shoulder. I smiled. It was the first real smile I had felt come over my face in years. I could see his monitor flashing orange. Orange meant it was over.

~ 3 ~

YELLOW

I stood back and watched the flames dance. Gold, sulfur, and citrine pixies waived their arms from high atop the remnants of my house. Their wings fluttered and shone brightly in the darkness of the night. The warmth from their glow was welcome as I stood in the gelidness of winter. A flaxen hue spread out over the snow-covered ground around me. I watched everything I owned burn and thought about the events that had led up to this moment.

I was an artist. I studied all of the greats and aspired to be one of them. I dabbled in many media except sculpture. I didn't feel myself entering my projects when I molded clay or chiseled rock. My true passion was painting and there wasn't much that I wouldn't try to turn into a work of art. As a child, my parents had a hard time keeping me from coloring on the walls and my teachers would chide me for the multi-colored doodles that accompanied my homework. Before I was a teenager, I had sanded and personalized every wooden piece of furniture in my room. My ceiling was a starlit sky with all of my favorite constellations. My walls were a jungle, a beach, mountains, and prairie fields. I had a small easel that I would take with me to the park or into the woods but my parents did not approve of me disappearing for long periods and at all hours of the day (I had to make sure I was there when the light was right). It was finally decided that my creativity needed an outlet and, more importantly, I needed a place to work where I couldn't, as my mother said, "create chaos or worry." So, they built a small studio in the garage for me. This was my heaven on earth, my Fortress of Solitude. I would still steal away occasionally to work outside, but the finishing touches were always done there.

This was where I had given life to the most important piece I had ever- and will ever- create. I remember how I felt as I dipped my brush and watched my canvas turn yellow. I like the color yellow. It is the color of friendship and peace. It represents enlightenment, loyalty, and joy. Whenever I used it in my artwork, no matter how bad a day I'd had, I would feel a wave of calm flow over me. I had been despondent for weeks over the sudden loss of my sister and decided to express myself to help me cope in the only way I knew how. I spent weeks on that canvas. Every shade had to be right. Every curve had to be perfect. The details could not be lost to any onlooker. I washed my brush a final time and stepped back. A single rose set in a sea of yellows. I had been careful to avoid too much green. It is the color of greed and my sister didn't have a greedy bone in her body. The cherry-red petal face looked back at me. I smiled.

My sister and I were very close in my childhood. We were separated by only a year of age and so remained best friends throughout our youth. We played together, went out on double dates together, and gossiped every night before bed. We talked about everything from school that day to future plans and dreams. Closer siblings could never have been found.

She had been taken from me and I never had a chance to prepare for it. It had been a stormy night. She had gone to the mall with her friends while our parents had taken men to help our grandparents move things from the attic. If I only had gone with her instead. Maybe I could have protected her or at least deterred the man who would be her murderer. She had been brutally attacked only a few months prior to the creation of my tribute and died before help could reach her. She was far too young for such a fate. At only eighteen years old, she had a beautiful life ahead of her that would never be lived. I looked at the rose. It was delicate and graceful, like her, and I paid tribute to her red hair in the colors I had chosen for the petals. I chose the yellow background, confident that she was at peace. I had painted this portrait as I remembered her. I spoke to it, softly. I told her how much I missed her. As I walked out of the garage, I took one last look back before turning out the light and shutting the door.

That night I couldn't rest. My mind kept going back to my sister's memorial, locked away in the cold garage. I slipped out of bed and tip-toed to the kitchen. As I passed the bookshelf in the living room, I saw her picture in the corner of my eye. I had never paid that close attention. There she was, in all her youth and beauty, bound in silver. I had taken that picture myself. We were younger- around fourteen and fifteen. Our parents had taken us to the zoo and allowed us to venture off on our own. We had fed the goats and flirted with the boy our age selling souvenirs. We had gorged on zebra ice cream; the remnants of which were on her lips in the picture. It had been a glorious day as just the two of us. I felt myself get misty-eyed at the memories.

I continued to the garage. I opened the door and flipped on the light. One of the bulbs failed to glow. There, in the dim light, the petals of the rose seemed to morph into the figure of her face. I stood transfixed by the sadness in her eyes.

If only I had been here that night. If only I had tagged along when you went to the mall like a good sister should have done. We had done everything together. Why not just that one night?

A sense of guilt overcame me and I felt my eyes sting from tears. It was my fault she had died so horribly. I had to have our parents take me to dinner after we'd left our grandparents' house, instead of coming straight home. She was eighteen and had just bought her own car. I thought she would want some time to show off to her friends away from her little sister. If I had gone with her or if my parents and I had come home instead of stopping to eat, she wouldn't have been alone. She would still be alive. As I knelt on the cold cement, I looked again at her sad face. I vowed to do whatever it took to live out her life's goals for her to the best of my ability. I was going to fulfill the dreams she didn't get the chance to. After I made my promise, I crept back to bed and quickly fell asleep.

I stayed true to my word. Over the next few

years, I applied myself harder than I ever knew I could. I moved her portrait to my bedroom so we could be closer. I told her everything. I complained about my teachers when I got home from school. I could hear her critiquing the boys I told her I liked and I would go over my homework with her. As I talked to her every night, gradually my guilt and sadness lifted. It didn't fully leave me, but it became a much lighter burden to bear.

I found a job studying paintings at the art museum and writing interpretations of them for the museum's magazine. I supplemented my income by selling some of my paintings to a local gallery. I moved down to the small town at the base of the violet-flowered hills where I grew up. My sister loved the hills where we were raised so I bought the first house I felt would do her justice. Even though I had a long commute, I couldn't bring myself to leave our little home. I set up my studio in the spare bedroom and placed her portrait high atop an easel in front of a window where she could see the rolling hills. We had a beautiful home, a career, and happiness. She only had one dream left for me to help her fulfill: marriage.

I had dated off and on through school and after. In my junior year of high school, the administration held a fundraiser allowing the kids to send roses to each other on valentine's day. My sister would have loved it. I was sure she would have had fifty roses compared to my three. That was when I had first realized our potential for loneliness. None of the relationships we entered seemed to last more than a few months. The men I felt myself drawn to were not ones I felt were suitable for me or my sister. My senior year, the boy I thought we might marry told me I needed to just move on from my sister's death. His friends had to pry my fingers from his throat and one of them sat on me until I calmed down. One man I met at the community college had seemed promising. I was very drawn to him and I loved the way he looked at me. I loved that he talked about our future together as if there were no questions in his mind. We were together for a little over a year before he let slip that he ultimately intended for me to give up my career to raise our future children. When I protested, he told me I should feel honored. After all, any other woman would be thrilled to have a future-wealthy man who wanted to take care of them. After more arguing, I not-so-politely told him where he could stuff his proposed future.

That night, I sat in front of my sister's portrait and recounted the fight word-for-word. She agreed that I had done the right thing and that he was not the right one for us. The yellow halo of canvas behind her created an aura of calm that washed over me. I pushed on with our search for Mr. Right. Some were handsome and some were intelligent, but none of them was everything we needed. We did manage to bring one consistent male into our lives. That wonderful cur protected our home and kept my sister company while I was at work. He was a great listener and we enjoyed watching TV together. Had he been human, he would have been perfect.

One day, a good friend from the museum and I decided to step out to lunch together. There was a great little bistro on the river and it wasn't too far from the museum. We were giggling about an attractive new intern and I spilled exaggerated woes of my love life when she suddenly stopped and got a serious smile on her face. She asked me if she could set me up with her brother. When I asked her what he was like, she said one simple word — rich.

I looked at her, dumbfounded by the answer. I flashed back to my former sweetheart. Why did it have to boil down to money? I felt the anger I had the last time I saw him return.

"What does money have to do with anything? Why do women want poetry, jewelry, expensive dinners, etcetera? Isn't love enough? It sometimes seems that the women around me don't believe that their man loves them unless he is going bankrupt trying to please her. Valentine's Day is the worst. On February fifteenth they cluster together and compare their plunder. Inevitably, the one with the engagement ring wins. If not her, then the one with the next most expensive piece of jewelry. Why? She'll only wear it once then it will get tucked away in a box with gifts of the past. When did romance get confused with expense? Give me a moonlit picnic followed by cuddling in front of a good movie. I would rather have a memory of true happiness than a necklace I'll wear once and probably forget about. I want love, not money. Is that so much to ask?"

I suddenly became aware of the fact that I was almost yelling. I looked around the restaurant and a hundred strange and wide-eyed faces stared at me. I felt absolutely humiliated and promptly left. I didn't want to be a trophy and I certainly didn't want to be a pet. We needed a husband, not a keeper. That night, my sister calmed me down and convinced me to apologize to my friend.

Despite my simple demands of men, I had very little luck in romance. Of all the things I looked for, money was not looked at in high regard. I was financially capable of taking care of myself and I took pride in that. I was still quite young but decided to temporarily set aside the hunt for a husband for my sister. They say the deer comes when the hunter stops looking. So, of course, that's when I met *him*.

I was standing outside of the coffee shop I visited every morning on my way to work. It was a beautiful, sunny day. I had my headphones on while listening to Scriabin's *Sonata Number Five* which had tuned out the rest of the world. He had put his hand on my shoulder to get my attention. I was so struck by his handsome face that I almost dropped my cell phone. He had just moved here and was looking for someone kind enough to give him directions to the hospital where he was to begin work as the new medical examiner. Being in the city, finding someone decent enough to extend such a simple courtesy as giving directions was extremely difficult. He said that I had a kind face so he thought I might be good enough to help him. Flattery combined with those beautiful brown eyes and broad shoulders overcame me and I offered him a ride. We did a great deal of talking in that less than ten-minute trip.

I thought he was rather naive and very trusting to accept a ride from a stranger. I told him he was lucky I wasn't one of those crazy people you heard about who picks up hitchhikers and cuts them up only to leave the corpses scattered along the countryside. He told me I seemed too sweet to do something so evil. He then proceeded to point out that he could just as easily have been a killer and I had openly allowed him in my car. Point taken.

As he got out of the car he smiled and winked a little as he said thank you. I pulled away, grinning like a child at Christmas. I was completely cloud-worthy for the rest of the day as I thought of the dark-haired stranger. My friend even commented that I had a particular glow and asked me to tell her all about him. There wasn't much to tell. I didn't even know his name.

That night, after work, I rushed home to tell my sister all about it. The rose looked back at me. She was obviously excited and happy for me. I told her I hoped to see him again and she approved.

The next morning, I was walking into the coffee shop again and saw a familiar face.

"If I didn't know better, I would think I had a stalker," I said as I took the latte he handed me.

"I thought we could walk a few blocks together today."

Leaving my car in the lot, we walked towards the hospital. With each step, we got further in-depth about our lives. Careers, hopes, dreams... it all came flooding out as if we had known each other before. When we arrived at the hospital, he put both of his arms around me. He smiled and the corners of his lips twitched a little. He wanted to kiss me. My entire body was invigorated with anticipation.

"What are you doing for dinner tonight?" He asked.

"I had planned a spaghetti dinner with Vinny."

He backed away a little. "Who is Vinny?"

"The love of my life." I smiled. "My dog."

An apparent wave of relief flowed over him. "Do you think he would mind if you made other arrangements?"

I spent a second day with my feet hardly touching the ground and my head in the clouds.

We had a lovely dinner at a cozy little Mexican restaurant. He opened the conversation by telling me that he had a confession. He told me he wasn't lost the day before; he just wanted an excuse to talk to me. He hadn't expected me to offer him a ride. He said after I had dropped him off, he had felt such a connection to me that he knew he had to see me again. Thoroughly flattered, I told him his behavior was forgiven.

Despite our conversation that day, he was very inquisitive about my job and my family. I openly told him about the two-hundred-year-old samples I was working on for the museum. I even told him about how my sister was bludgeoned to death that terrible night and how connected she and I were. I couldn't stop myself. It was as if just being near him made me want to tell our life story. The entire time I talked, those perfect brown eyes never left mine. I was mesmerized by them, I'm sure. They were as hypnotic as a magician's pendulum. When I asked him about his family, he didn't say much. He told me he was the normal one and that if I ever met them to stay away from his brother with the green eyes.

We went back to his apartment for a nightcap and I admittedly had more than one. He offered to let me stay and sleep it off. We lay in his bed. His warm breath was on my neck, his arm wrapped around me, and his thumb gently caressing my stomach. I would gladly have spent the rest of my life reliving those moments. His heartbeat against my spine; a quick, almost nervous, yet hypnotic rhythm. I took a deep breath. When he kissed my neck, my entire body felt exhilarated and peaceful in the same instant. I love that feeling.

It was passionate excellence. Our bodies moved as if performing an intricate dance. When it was over, I sat in his lap for a few moments, still shaking from the events of the past hour. He looked up at me and smiled. His powerful arms reached up and pulled me against his chiseled chest. That night I slept- truly slept- for the first time in months. That was it, the beginning of the end. We were inseparable from that day on.

He was amazing in every way a man could be. He listened to my every word as if it were life-giving air. He praised my talents as if I were Gentileschi herself. He was contributory instead of controlling. He was intelligent. He was charming. He was gorgeous. He was perfection in its purest form. I gladly made my friends jealous when we went out for drinks. I could not have been happier.

Every night I came home and told my sister all about him. She stared back approvingly. She was proud of our success and happiness. The first night he stayed at our house, I had introduced them. He seemed to only see a canvas with a rose. I was disheartened by that. They were the two most important people in my life. After he had gone the following morning, I went to my studio and sought her guidance. She helped me understand that the bond she and I shared was unique and while he didn't understand it, he didn't ridicule it either and I should not rush to judge a fish that cannot fly.

I took my sister's advice and we continued to date. I felt myself falling more deeply in love with him. I only spoke of my sister in fond memories instead of as the part of me she was. It felt like a betrayal, but she assured me she felt no such thing and she understood it was necessary. The months rolled by quickly. As I sat at lunch with my friends one day, I was bragging about the flowers my Love had given me the previous night. Our anniversary was drawing near and he was treating me like a goddess. I refused to acknowledge that part of me had become one of the women I had often criticized as I admitted that I was secretly hoping he was going to ask me to marry him. It was the only dream my sister had left.

My best friend looked at me and put her hand on my shoulder. "Love is like a tornado. You can get caught up in it, you can't control it, and if you aren't careful, it can ruin your life."

I stared at her blankly. I had no idea what she was talking about. I was happy. I was truly happy.

"What is that supposed to mean?" I asked.

"It's barely been a year. Maybe you should slow down a bit?"

"Why? He's perfect and we're happy. He's everything we've been looking for."

"What do you mean 'we?'"

Infuriated, I told her I didn't owe her any explanation. We were perfect together and that was all that mattered.

A week later I came home from work. I was exhausted. The museum was keeping me very busy. I unlocked the door and stepped into what should have been a dark entryway. Instead, there was a path of yellow rose petals lined with tea-light candles. I smiled. It was our anniversary. I followed the path down the hall and into the bathroom. The tub was overflowing with scented bubbles. Soft music was playing and honey candles were lined on every available surface. I giggled a little. I knew normal men don't really do things like this, but I didn't care. I was exhausted and those bubbles were far too enticing. I eagerly stripped down and slipped into the tub. It was sensationally relaxing. Lavender and honey scents carried my mind away as I allowed the warmth of the water to relax my stress-filled muscles.

As I lay back in the tub playing with the warm bubbles, I noticed the back of the door. The most beautiful black satin gown hung on a hanger. Sticking to the front was a small note that read simply "wear me." I smiled and dunked my head under the water. When I surfaced, I watched the flames on the candles dance and the yellow wax drip down the sides. Yellow roses. Yellow candles. Yellow is such a calming color. He knew me so well and I felt showered with affection as I basked in my favorite color. I breathed deeply, taking in as much of the honey aroma as I could.

I stayed in the water as long as I could

without my skin getting wrinkled. When I finally forced myself to climb out, I let the water out of the tub and toweled off. I did the best I could to fix my hair and make myself appear worthy of the obviously expensive dress that had been left for me.

When I left the bathroom, a new path had been created out of the rose petals and candles. I stepped lightly. The flowers tickled my still-naked feet. It led down the hall and out into the backyard. I slid the glass door open. There he stood. The chiminea was ablaze. Yellow and red roses were everywhere. A soft melody played from the radio he had tried to hide with the flowers. The table for two was laden with candles and petals. In the middle of it all, he stood, dressed in his best, and grinning broadly. Even Vinny wore a bowtie and sat wagging his tail happily.

I walked up to him and kissed him passionately. He seated me at the table and began to serve me sesame chicken and fried rice from a bowl. He couldn't cook, but he knew my favorite foods. I didn't have the heart to tell him I knew he couldn't cook and I had seen the remnants of the Chinese takeout containers burning in the chiminea.

"This is all too much." I smiled.

"A special dinner for a special occasion." He smiled back and seated himself.

His words struck me. A special occasion. This was it. He was going to ask for my hand. I felt giddy and lightheaded. I glanced at the house and could see my sister watching through the window.

All through dinner I waited anxiously. I ate carefully though quickly (I was very hungry). If the ring was hidden in my food, I didn't want to ingest it. He spoke of the usual things, work, family, etcetera. When was he going to do it? If I had to wait much longer, I thought I was going to jump out of my skin.

After dinner, he stood and asked me to dance. This was it. He pulled me close to him. He pressed his forehead against mine as we floated across the scattered petals on the patio. The dance led us into the bedroom. After the flurry of delight, he lay holding me in his arms. His naked skin was warm against mine. His heartbeat was quick and excited.

"I love you," he whispered.

"I love you too," I whispered back.

This was it!

"I think we should live together."

He was going to do it! "I think we should too."

He smiled. "Then it's settled. We will move my things this weekend."

Just a minute. That was it? He just wanted to live together? What about marriage? I rolled and volleyed this information in my head until he fell asleep.

After I was sure he was snoring, I put on my robe and tiptoed to my studio. My sister was there waiting. I was frustrated. I began to tell her about what happened. I wanted him to ask me. This was all I needed to make her life complete. My sister looked disapproving as I ranted about how wonderful and yet maddening the whole night had been. I would have mentioned marriage but I didn't wish to seem too eager. My sister found that very amusing.

I stroked the peaceful yellow background of the canvas. She calmed me and explained that my friend had been right. I was trying to move things too quickly and I needed to take a step back. Living together was the obvious next step and it was one stride closer to our end goal. There was nothing wrong with living together; it just didn't feel like it was quite enough. We had only been together for a year anyway. Why had I gotten my hopes up so much? If you don't get your hopes up, you can't be disappointed. But then, what do you have to look forward to? What is the point of aspiring to do better or to be better? It's a driving force and disappointment is necessary to force us to want better or try harder. But we must be careful to never confuse want with need. Being disappointed about what one wants is very different from being disappointed about what one needs. I didn't just want to marry him. I *needed* to. I was just going to have to settle for the new living arrangement and be happy with that. I said goodnight to my sister and went back to bed.

That weekend, we rented a truck and began to pack up his apartment. He really didn't have much in his one-bedroom flat. We had agreed to use his bed instead of mine as it was bigger but to keep my dining set. Having planned ahead made the day run smoothly. Friends joined in and loaded their cars with boxes. It was a day-long affair. As we passed each other, we would sneak a kiss here and there. It was very reassuring. I had since come to terms with what was happening and even looked forward to it. No, it wasn't marriage, but it was close enough for now.

That night, we opened a bottle of wine in celebration and sipped as we unpacked his things. Vinny randomly stuck his head in boxes and sniffed the items removed from them. As we worked, we talked about our new life together. He spoke of how wonderful it will be to wake up to me every morning. We would no longer meet at the coffee shop every morning to walk to work. We could have a real breakfast together every day. I loved hearing him talk like that. Maybe a wedding wasn't too far in our future after all.

The next morning, I woke to the smell of fresh coffee and scrambled eggs. I walked out into the kitchen. He smiled and pulled a chair out for me. We had a pleasant breakfast and showered together before work. I was going to be spoiled if he kept this up.

The next few months were everything he promised and more. We had breakfast and dinner together every day. After rough days at work, he would sit on the couch watching television with me and rubbing my shoulders. It was paradise. Yet, with all this affection, he still had not asked me to marry him. Every night after he fell asleep, I would slip back to my studio and confide in my sister. A few times, I thought I saw him watch me get out of bed, but he never mentioned it. She would stare back at me, night after night. Knowing that she was there to talk to was a great comfort. She guided me and reminded me to remain patient with him.

I was patient, but that didn't stop me from dropping hints. We would stroll through the store and I would happen to mention how lovely a particular ring looked. When we watched television together and saw a wedding scene, I would comment about how I envied the beautiful bride and was excited to one day be in her shoes. He would make a slight giggle and tell me that someday it would happen. But as the days rolled on, I began to wonder.

One night, I came home from work late. I

had been forced to work on a Saturday and a blizzard just happened to roll in. My Love had called me and told me the power was out. He said he could see his breath inside the house and Vinny was huddled up against him under the blanket. I told him he could burn the damaged canvases on the floor in my studio in the fireplace once the dry wood we had stored ran out. Vinny had run through my studio chasing a ball the day before. He had been confined indoors due to the cold for several days. He had a lot of energy that needed to be released so I could not be angry, but he knocked over and ruined several canvases and broke the easel that my sister resided on.

Finally, I was permitted to leave my office. The sun had long set, not that one could have seen it through the storm. The snow made visibility on the road nearly impossible. The streets were icy and slick in the hills outside the city. As I drove, I noticed that all the lights were low in the houses, and the street lamps were not lit. The power was still out.

I finally pulled into my driveway. As I walked in, the warmth from the fireplace hit me. It felt wonderful. Vinny ran to greet me. Candles were lit on the mantel, end tables, and throughout the dining room. My Love sat on the couch with two plates of cheese and two glasses of wine. It was just what I needed.

After we ate, I carried a candle to the bathroom and showered. There was thankfully some lukewarm water left in the tank. I toweled off and began to head towards the bedroom. I noticed that the door to my studio was still open. I carried the candle in. I was struck immediately. My sister was gone.

I stormed into the living room and confronted him angrily.

"Where is she?" I screamed.

"Who?"

He looked terrified and confused.

"My sister! Her painting was in my studio! What did you do with her?"

He looked at the fire. "You told me I could burn the canvases that were in there."

"Not that one! You killed her! You killed her again!"

Rage, despair, pain, and heartbreak all battled for control over me. I wanted to cry but there were no tears. I wanted to collapse but I wanted to lash out and hurt him. I could feel myself turning red and losing control.

"What are you talking about?" He stood and faced me.

"You know I lost my sister once and now you've killed her again!"

"I didn't mean to burn your painting. I misunderstood what you said on the phone. I didn't do it on purpose. I would never want to hurt you!"

"Obviously, that's a lie! You never asked me to marry you!"

"What does that have to do with any of this?"

"I promised my sister I would find a good man. She never had the chance to. I swore I would do it for her." I felt the tears finally come.

He paused. "Is that why you talk to yourself in the middle of the night?"

"I'm not talking to myself! I'm talking to my sister! I had to make sure she still approved of you even though you wouldn't marry her!"

"I never wanted to marry her. I didn't even know her! I want to spend my life with you!"

"I have to get married for her and she liked you!"

"Do you hear yourself? It's just a painting!"

"Just a painting? Just a painting! She was my sister!"

I shoved him as hard as I could. He fell backward into the fireplace. His cotton sweater lit up in a ball of flame. He screamed and fell to the floor. He rolled around on the carpet in an attempt to put the flames out. In my rage, I ran to my studio and grabbed my oil paints. I covered his writhing body in paint and acetone and fed the flames. He knocked over the candles as he flailed. The more he moved, the more the house caught fire. I suddenly realized what was happening. I grabbed Vinny and ran outside.

This is how I found myself there. I was standing barefoot in the snow, clutching my dog. I watched the yellow flames waltz and felt my pounding heart slowly settle. My sister had been stolen from me twice. My home and everything she and I owned were in flames. As I watched, I breathed deeply. My lover was dead.

I thought about my sister as I heard sirens in the background, just like the night they had come for her body so many years ago. Now I had to rebuild our home and everything we had created. I would have to find a new husband for us. Though my heart and mind should have been irreparably broken, I was strangely at ease. I would put paint to canvas again. I would give her life for the third time. I could almost see her face, smiling in approval at me from the flames as she had that first night I painted her portrait. Though our house was ablaze, we were strong enough to rebuild. The saffron-colored inferno reached toward heaven. Yellow is a color of optimism and remembrance. It's such a soothing color.

~ 4 ~

GREEN

Beware of the green-eyed monster. He is the embodiment of covetous and lust. He exerts his power over the weak, compelling them to commit crimes against their fellow man in the name of self-gratification. These behaviors, while initially resulting in false happiness, will ultimately be the victim's downfall.

Those who are strong of will and heart can resist his influence. While they may have moments of frailty, ultimately, their good nature will out. Those who succumb to him act purely in their own self-interest. Not even their family members are seen with a value equal to their own.

My mother was an extremely superstitious woman. She feared everything from black cats to the number thirteen. Even if a teacup breaks the wrong way, it may send her into a panic. Unfortunately, that superstitious nature extended to me as well. My eyes are a rare shade of true green; not the hazel color that is so often seen. She cried when I was born. They were not tears of joy. She had said that green-eyed boys were covetous and self-serving. She said that I had been tainted in the womb by the green-eyed monster himself. My father disagreed with her and he said that as long as they raised me right, everything would be fine. My existence became the source of a great deal of discord in their marriage. To my father's credit, he stood up for me where he could, but ultimately, his wife was stronger.

My mother was abhorrently adamant in her beliefs. She vehemently denied that it was possible for me to grow up to be a good man. My grandfather, her father, had green eyes. He was a family disgrace. He wanted very little to do with his siblings or even his progeny. He cared about two things- money and possessions. After my grandmother left him, he married a wealthy widow and kept her locked in the house where no one else could have any contact with her. He had completely isolated her from her children and family. Officially, his suspicious death was ruled a suicide, but my mother never believed it. Some in the family think his second wife either in an act of self-preservation or malice, had killed him. There was no note and no weapon found to create the slashes on his wrists. The family knew the generations-old jewelry box in which she kept a sapphire-handled knife but they all felt he had received his just reward.

My mother hissed at me that I would get my comeuppance, just as her grandfather had. I was doomed to inherit his lust and avarice; it was only a matter of time. Other than the clear disdain my mother harbored toward me (for something that was completely out of my control), I had a normal childhood. We lived deep in the heart of suburbia in a modest middle-class house. I went to school, took piano lessons, and played baseball. I was a straight-A student. I had plenty of friends growing up. We always played either outside or at their houses. I was never lonely but I still felt alone. I think there was a piece missing from my life... a mother's love. Nothing was unusual about me but I could tell that my mother saw my good grades and social grace as a charade. She believed I was only attempting to mask my "true nature." She treated me much differently from my two brown-eyed brothers. They never received evil looks whenever something went wrong and whenever they wanted something, their wishes were granted. If I wanted something, it was the monster of greed I held within me rearing his ugly head.

For example, when I was a teenager, I wanted a car for my birthday. My brothers had each received one and I thought it was fair to ask. I did get a car. While they had each received gently used but clean and well-running vehicles, the day before my birthday, a tow truck pulled into the driveway hauling a filthy white, decade-old hatchback with dry rotted tires, a blown motor, and dented body panels. My mother said that I needed to understand how to work for what I wanted. She made me repair it with my own money. My brothers laughed as if it were funny. My father said I was lucky to have received a car at all. He told me my mother didn't want to get me one because it would be enforcing my selfish behavior. He fought her on the issue but he was a weak willed man and so a shell of an automobile was a great victory.

While comfortably social with my male peers, I do not know if my own awkwardness towards the fairer sex stemmed from my father's weakness or my mother's power. Whichever it was, it lasted the better part of my life. I did not date very often. I had a difficult time gathering up the courage to face a woman and if I did manage to take her out, silence encapsulated our evening. I didn't give up per se, but I grew more discouraged with each encounter. Needless to say, I spent the bulk of my high school and college years alone.

I was a fervent reader my whole life. I think it was because I was so deeply displeased with the negative treatment from my mother and so I was with many aspects of my life. Despite my outward behavior, I lived in constant fear of not only failure but that I may somehow one day prove her right. Since boys didn't discuss such things and I had no female counterpart, I kept these feelings to myself. I frequently daydreamed and filled countless journals. I think I just needed to separate the stable part of my mind from my less composed psyche. Sometimes it was hard to differentiate between the two. It felt so liberating to get lost in someone else's imagination. I must admit, I frequently indulged in adult romance novels. The lust and passion exhilarated me. I enjoyed those that included murder and crime the most. It fed my yearning for freedom from my unhappy world. I could never imagine myself harming someone, fantasy was the release that sated me.

The more I aged, the worse it became. I was frequently tired. I wished there was a switch on the side of my head that I could use to turn my brain off. When I had nothing profound to think about, I would daydream. Most of the time I didn't have any control over what I thought about. It was kind of scary when I would drive and end up someplace with no conception of how I got there. I would lay in bed at night-awake but asleep. I had no idea what was going on around me as I was dead to the world but my mind was reeling with some fantasy that would undoubtedly become another entry in my journal.

I decided that if I couldn't turn my brain off, I would use it. I went to college and majored in creative writing. I ended up getting a job writing for a competitive magazine in the city. I loved my job. I always had my assignments turned in early. I couldn't turn my brain off, what else was I going to do?

One Christmas, my entire family gathered for a feast. This was not an annual occurrence as my extended family lived out of state. My Aunt and uncle piled armfuls of gifts under the tree. My oldest brother brought his artistic young girlfriend. The younger of the two came alone, as always. He sat at the far end of the dinner table, smiling quietly to himself, and stirring his mashed potatoes. I didn't like the way he was smiling. Something about it made me very uneasy.

My aunt suddenly spoke. "So, does anyone have any new news?"

My younger brother spoke for the first time

that evening. "I have a girlfriend," he continued to poke at his food and smile.

"Really? Why didn't you bring her to meet us?" my aunt asked.

"Dolls don't count." My older brother laughed.

"She couldn't come. She was going out of town to see her family." My younger brother looked up sharply.

"Where did you two meet?" My aunt continued her line of inquiry.

"At the little bistro on the river."

"Congratulations. I can't wait to meet her." My aunt raised her glass.

"And you're still alone?" My mother turned to me.

"I just haven't found my someone yet." I looked down at my plate.

"I'm sure." My mother sounded less than convinced.

"Why kind of pie do we have?" I smiled at my father in gratitude for changing the subject.

We continued the festivities. We tore into our gifts as if we were still children. My brothers each received the latest in techno-whatever and gift cards to nice restaurants. My aunt and uncle gifted me a nice new leather journal. Fortunately, my family did not feel the same way about me as my mother. She, as with each year, presented me with new socks (not from a thrift store this year!) My father, having known what his in-laws had chosen, gifted me a beautiful new pen set. My mother's eyes shot daggers into him as she apparently had been unaware of the gift. Overall, it was a good Christmas.

That night, back in my own home, my cat lay on my chest in bed and stared at me. I began to feel guilty about not asking my younger brother more questions about his girlfriend. This was a big deal for him. He probably wanted to sing it from the mountains and we all went on with other things. We had never been close growing up. Mother's preferential treatment had seen to that. But he was still my brother. Hell, maybe he had some good advice for me.

My cat's glare reminded me that my father had always wanted us to look out for each other. But I knew why I hadn't asked. It wasn't fair. Why should he find love and not me? I tried to and couldn't find anyone to love me. He was a do-nothing and yet he could be happy? It just wasn't fair. I thought about meeting this young woman and maybe that would make me feel better about the situation. I shook off the idea. I grew tired and began to get angry at the guilt my cat was instilling in me. I pushed her off the bed, rolled over, and went to sleep.

When Mother died, I should have felt something. My brothers were both devastated and my father was virtually destroyed. As we carried her casket, they all tried to control their tears, to be the strong men who didn't show their heartache. I didn't have to try. I felt nothing. I knew a part of me would miss her. She was my mother, after all. But my conscience was clear and my heart intact. When my father had told me a week before that he found her body on the bathroom floor, I didn't shed one salty drop. I was sure it was her own bitterness that had eaten her core that had caused her unexpected death. As I watched her casket being lowered into the earth, I secretly hoped the hole had been dug deep enough to reach straight to Hell.

After Mother had been sent to the Eternal fire, life continued as usual. Every night I would go to bed alone and wake up the same way. I began to loathe the idea of ever falling in love. It seemed that my cat was the only one capable of true affection for me. I became increasingly bitter. I avoided the women at work. I hated them all. It was as if I was some kind of sick joke to them all.

Then, we hired HER.

Towards early spring, work was rushed. Busy people were bustling about the office. Rumors of a complete takeover were spreading like wildfire and everyone was on edge. For those who had been with the magazine from the beginning, it signaled the end of an era. Those who had recently joined feared their careers to be cut before they had a chance to begin. They were incredibly uneasy days but we still found a way to make the work a little more enjoyable through laughter and good friendships that had developed. While I felt somewhat well-liked, I didn't have any close friends but everyone else was able to lean on each other for comfort and their energy made everything more bearable for the rest of us.

I was in my mid-twenties at the time. It was

a Tuesday. I loved Tuesdays. She was in the office on that day every week at nine sharp. After our first meeting, I inquired about her from rumormongers at work. She was a freelance field writer. She only came in on Tuesdays because that was when her weekly column was due so it could go to press and be released by Friday. She was single and lived alone. She had a passion for the environment, which was the focus of her column.

She was perfect. She was grace in the very depiction of the word. Her long slender legs stretched gracefully upward to neatly rounded hips. Her waist tucked inward gently beneath her ribs. Her breasts were round and firm. Her arms were delicate but defined and stretched to porcelain hands and lacy fingertips. Her neck was a lovely pedestal for a work of art. She was Aphrodite herself. She walked with distinct poise and purpose. Every movement she made was as delicate and striking as butterfly wings. Her soft brown hair moved like ocean waves.

Her smile could bring joy to an entire room and she was always happy to see me. She was in love with me; I could see the desire fervently ablaze in her eyes. Her eyes! They were almost as green as my own. They burned with passion and desire. They were two emeralds in a porcelain setting. Green for avarice- the true color of passion. They looked into my own with such longing it was impossible to ignore.

Having virtually no experience with women, I only had my books as references to her behavior and our interaction. I studied her carefully. Sometimes I would get close enough to smell her. She smelled like a spring meadow. Her laugh was a musical note, not like the other women in the office who sounded like high-pitched mules. Her house was painstakingly kept on the outside. The flower beds were a tidy compilation of colors that perfectly complimented each other. Her grass was trimmed and her shutters had a clean coat of paint. She even had a white picket fence. I don't know what the inside looked like since I couldn't see it from the street, but I had no doubt it was just as well kept as the outside. Everything about her exuded class and sophistication and the more I learned, the more I wanted to know.

She wanted me. I wanted her. My heart

would thunder in my chest whenever I caught her stealing a peek at me from a stack of papers she so inconspicuously hid behind. Those eyes. I wanted to put them on my wall and keep them for myself so they could never gaze upon anyone else. No. I wanted to keep them in a box. Then no one could look at my treasure. They would be there only for me. My secret jewels. I knew she felt the same way about me. Those eyes told me everything I needed to know. She had been born with desire and, in that moment, I was the object of that yearning. She would never tell me. We merely exchanged courtesies and went about our work, but I knew she was in love with me. She was just waiting for the right time to tell me.

I tried on several occasions to ask her to dinner or even strike up a general conversation with her. I could feel the eyes of my coworkers burning into me and, unsurprisingly, my gawky habits from my younger years would shine through and I would make up an excuse to walk away from her. I could hear my coworker's snickers. They whispered words like 'awkward' and 'nerdy.' It was all right, though. I knew she would come to me when she was ready.

One particular Tuesday, she came up to me just as I was leaving for lunch. She asked if I could give her a ride to the burger joint up the road because her car was in the shop. I gladly agreed. This was it; she was finally going to confess her deep emotional attachment to me. This was my big chance. We would be away from the undeniable gossips at work and alone together.

As we sat in the drive-thru, she was quiet. I decided to try and make things a little easier on her. I thought maybe if I opened the gates of conversation a little, the flood of emotion and longing she had for me would pour out. My heart skipped three beats as I tried desperately to think of what to say.

"I'm glad you asked for a ride," I said as coolly as I could.

She smiled. "I'm glad you let me tag along. Everyone else had already gone to lunch."

There was a little more awkward silence.

"You know, you really are quite beautiful," I said, hearing the nervousness in my voice.

She shifted in her seat a little. "That's very sweet of you to say."

I was unsure how to break the tension. I unbuckled my seatbelt so I could turn to face her better. Her eyes widened and she shifted in her seat again. I took her squirming as a sign that she was just nervous about her imminent confession. I wanted so desperately to show her that her feelings were mutual. I wanted her to know that I yearned for her as much as she did for me. I leaned over and began to kiss her neck. She moved closer to the window. I moved with her and continued kissing and gently rubbed the inside of her leg.

"What are you doing?!" she looked horrified.

I felt stunned for a moment. "This is what you wanted, isn't it? Why you asked me to take you out?"

"What? No!" she pushed me back.

How could she tell me no? She loved me! I knew she did! A great rage boiled inside of me. I ignored the food and drove her back to work. She rushed to get out of the car. I watched as she swiped her badge quickly and pushed her way through the revolving door. She said no! I threw the car into gear and drove home, knowing that I wasn't supposed to leave work yet. I didn't care. She couldn't say no! It was her idea! She was going to confess her love for me! I paced through every room in my house until morning. I didn't eat or sleep that night. I was fueled entirely by emotion.

As the sun rose, I watched my cat perched in the window. She was eagerly stalking a blue jay at the feeder on the other side of the glass. I felt myself smile at how silly she was. She knew she couldn't catch that bird. She knew the glass was there. Yet, she still tried to stalk it and imagined her victory.

As I drove back to work, I continued to contemplate the events of the previous day and began to ask questions. Why do we always not just want what we *don't* have but what we *can't* have? Is it because desire is the driving force of successful species? I thought about my cat and the jay. She had all of the food, toys, and treats she could possibly want right at the tips of her claws but yet, she wanted that jay. It was that forbidden thing that she could not have. She stalked, stared, and chirped, but she knew she could never reach it. But still, she dreamed of the day it would be hers.

That was it! My emerald-eyed Aphrodite thought she *couldn't* have me. That's why she was so deeply in love with me! I was her blue bird! I was just on the other side of a great barrier that she didn't think she could break through. It was the only logical explanation. Why else would she watch me from across the room, only to avert her gaze when our eyes met? Why else would she have asked me to take her to lunch? I didn't understand what barrier she could perceive but it was real enough to her. I decided to encourage her. If she realized she could have me, maybe she would take more initiative.

The following Tuesday I found her alone in the copy room. She was wearing my favorite blue skirt; the one without the pinstripes. She was also wearing her hair down. I loved it when she did that.

Too dumbstruck by her beauty to think of anything profound, I stood in the doorway and simply said "hi."

She wheeled around and clutched her

papers to her chest. "Uh. Hi." She smiled but it wasn't her usual warm, happy smile.

"I didn't mean to startle you." I stepped towards her.

She stepped back, still clutching her papers. "That's okay."

"I realize I may have put you off at lunch last week but I was wondering if you might like to try dinner sometime?" I had come completely into the room with her.

"Oh. Uh. Look, you seemed like a nice enough guy and I thought you were pretty harmless but I just don't think it's a good idea."

As she was talking, she had been steadily maneuvering closer to the door until she finally said, "I'm sorry," and ducked out

I watched her go. She called me a 'nice guy.' That was proof that she liked me. Maybe I had just come on too strong and needed to give her the chance to make her move at her own pace. But I couldn't back own. I couldn't let her think that I had lost interest or, God forbid, that I was going to give up on us.

I repeatedly asked her to let me take her out to dinner. I text messaged her phone and said she was beautiful and sexy and told her that she was my everything. Every Tuesday I pushed a little further. I would rub her shoulders as she sat at her computer and gave her hips a loving squeeze when she stood.

On nights I couldn't sleep, I'd sit in my car across the street and hope she would sense my presence and take comfort in it. Sometimes there was a blue BMW in her driveway. It would stay there until morning when a blonde man, usually wearing a nice suit, would leave. I had to quelch my jealousy and remind myself it was probably her brother. She was not the kind of woman who would cheat on me and I had overheard her telling a coworker that her brother was a tall blonde. Still, I was not heartbroken when the BMW stopped making appearances.

I opened the gates as far as I could. I gave her every opportunity to admit her feelings for me. She was just too shy. But I still saw that same desire in those flawless bottle-green eyes and it gave me the strength to continue encouraging her. Every time I saw her watching me from across the room or when she 'accidentally' changed her arrival time to match mine, I knew we were on similar pages in the novella that was our romance.

One day, my editor called me into his office. He told me there had been complaints about my 'lewd' behavior. Human Resources had wanted to formally reprimand me but he felt it was something we could settle ourselves. Apparently, some woman had written a complaint against me. He wouldn't give me a name but it was obvious that some woman either jealous of my Aphrodite or worse, some man jealous of the attention she was giving me had written the complaint. They claimed inappropriate physical and verbal behavior on my part. This wretched person had gone so far as to request my termination or reassignment. I was told not to touch any female coworkers and watch what I say. I listened as I was told to either tone down my behavior or it could cost me my job.

As I walked out of his office, I saw her standing near the fax machine. Her eyes burned. I knew she couldn't have been the one to file the complaints against me. She wanted me too badly.

I was becoming increasingly frustrated. Every

morning I watched my cat stalk the bird outside the window. I was that bird. I knew the predator was there but I also knew there was something I couldn't see keeping her from me.

It was raining as I left work one dark Tuesday night. I was working on an extra project, trying to get back in my editor's good graces. After our discussion, I felt like not only he, but many of the other men in the office looked at me differently. As I left through the back door near the loading dock, I caught a glimpse of something in the shadows. The loading dock should have been empty. We had laid off the night shift loaders due to budget cuts. I squinted my eyes in the darkness and moved closer. It was her. She saw me and took a small step back. I smiled and walked up to her. She was soaked to the bone and shivering.

"Why are you standing out in the rain?" I asked.

"I'm still having car trouble. My taxi will be here soon," she replied.

"Well, I can give you a lift. Save you some money."

She shook her head. "My taxi will be here soon," she repeated. "Thank you," she added.

I tried to keep her engaged in conversation. "Your brother can't pick you up in the beamer?"

Her eyes, those beautiful orbs, widened. "That's not—" she stopped. "My taxi will be here soon." She said for the third time.

I felt all of the anger and hurt and frustration I had been shoving inside start to boil until it just erupted.

"I have given you every opportunity to tell me how much you love me and still you refuse to take it!" I heard myself yell. "Why?!"

She looked horrified. "What are you talking about? I don't love you!"

She lied! Was this a sick game to her? How could she do this to me? I grabbed her throat and slammed her against the cement wall.

"Don't lie to me!"

"I'm not lying! What are you talking about? Are you insane? Let go!"

Her words spoke denial but I could see that desire in those eyes. It was more intense than I had ever known it to be. I pressed my lips against hers. She bucked away and kicked me in the knee. I fell to the ground. She ran for the door. I grabbed her just as she grasped for her security badge to let herself back into the building. She kicked and screamed. I cupped my hand over her mouth. She bit me. I threw her. The sharp crack of the lightning above could not mask the dull thud her head made as it hit the pavement. She lay motionless in a puddle. Suddenly, our little dispute only seconds ago meant nothing.

I couldn't believe it. I had hurt her. I had hurt the only woman who had ever loved me. What had I done? I carefully scooped her up and carried her to my car. I laid her carefully across the back seat. I drove her to my home, wishing I hadn't harmed her.

I laid her on my bed and undressed her. Her alabaster skin was flawless. I smiled at the thought that this beautiful creature loved me. She lay naked on my silk bedspread as I toweled the rain from her body and mopped the blood from her forehead. She was perfection. I ran my fingers over her soft skin. I felt the hair on the back of my neck stand on end. I took a deep breath and forced myself to move away from her.

I bandaged up my bite wound before I cooked myself dinner and fed my cat. I walked back into my bedroom. She hadn't moved. I put my hand on her cheek. She was a little chilly. I moved her gently and pulled the bed coverings over her. I undressed and slid into the bed next to her. I lay there staring at her perfection. In that moment, I forgave her for all of the frustration she had put me through in the prior months. She was worth it. I sighed and smiled. I wrapped my arm around her and went to sleep a happy man.

The next morning, I roused early. I looked over at her sleeping body. She needed her rest. I'm sure the emotional outburst from the previous night had drained her. I walked out to the living room and rubbed my eyes. My cat lay on the coffee table. That wasn't her usual morning perch. I looked out the window. The bird wasn't at the feeder. I shrugged my shoulders and walked into the kitchen for breakfast. After a good bowl of oatmeal, I showered again and dressed for work. I went back to the bedroom. She still lay asleep. I kissed her forehead. She still felt cold. I pulled another blanket on top of her and left for work.

~ 5 ~

BLUE

Blue is a cold color not only in the spectrum but in our language. Someone unhappy or depressed is said to be blue. Blue is the color of dejection and desolation. One color with multiple meanings, all with sad connotations. I think I understand why.

The pavement was cold that morning as I walked home barefoot; my remaining shoe clutched loosely in my left hand. It was October and the leaves were falling all around like a beautiful rain of red and cold. A cold gust of wind sent a chill up my skirt. The sun was just beginning to peer over the purple horizon. I loved this time of the morning when the night was fading and birds were waking.

I stared at the ground with a smile on my face as I shuffled along, trying to keep my bare legs warm. It was a futile effort since the frigid cement beneath my feet had already numbed my toes. As I watched each step before I took it, I noticed a tiny blue butterfly. Its bright cerulean wings were frozen to the ground. I stopped and stared at the insect. I felt my heart sink. Frosted to the ground before me was a metaphor for the woman I used to be. I had been trapped and dead inside just like this poor creature. Once upon a time, we had been happy. It felt like another life. Long ago, my heart would skip a beat and I had figurative butterflies inside me every time he looked at me or our hands touched. Once upon a time…

I had been sitting on a blanket at the park enjoying a steamy romance novel. The sun had been warm and the air was clear. I'd needed a break from my college studies and escaped to the outdoors and into a world that would make my ancestors blush. Being completely engrossed in the pages before me, I didn't hear the stomping feet approaching me. I didn't even know anyone was nearby until another body collided with mine.

I heard a voice I didn't recognize. "I'm so sorry! Are you all right?"

Stunned, it took me a moment to realize what had happened. I looked up at the handsome, red-haired stranger. He was tall and well-built. His hair and goatee were neatly trimmed. His eyes were soft and concerned. His muscular arm extended a strong hand down to me to help me to my feet. And such was the beginning of our story.

When we had started dating everything was magic. Not to sound melodramatic, but I felt so much like royalty when we were together, that I could have made Hera, the queen of queens herself, envious. He was funny and witty and charming. The way he had looked at me made me feel like I was the only thing that mattered in his world. Expensive dinners, gifts of clothes and jewelry, forehead kisses, and passionate nights together were the norm and I was happy.

I miss the romance. Not even the big stuff; I prefer simplicity in my life. I miss the little things that mean so much to me. I don't need a seventy-dollar steak dinner when a forty-dollar one would do. Jewelry was only expected on holidays, not just random Wednesdays. Massages and weekends away meant far more than destination vacations. In the beginning, I would make my friends jealous with my stories of the sweet little nothings he used to do for me. The flowers, the backrubs... all of it.

But it's gone now. No more tenderness. No more romantic touches. Now he's become every other scrotum-scratching, belching, beer-guzzling Neanderthal I have ever dated. It's almost as if as soon as he realized he had won my heart, he no longer had a need to make me feel special. I longed for those strong hands on my back and shoulders and the 'I love you' that was once said with such emotion and fervor. But no more. It's all gone. Even the passion from his lips as they press against mine. It is now a completely obligatory gesture. My heart aches to have that back. He seemed to turn from prince to toad in the blink of an eye. I had not intended to find my butterflies elsewhere. I had consigned myself to misery. The Fates had other plans. This is how I found myself walking along a cold sidewalk, barely dressed, and still reeling about the events of the night before.

My new prince and I had met some time ago through a mutual friend. The first night we had spent together was incredible. His lips were soft, his eyes were warm, and his vigor was unforgettable. The next morning was slightly awkward. I had stayed for a little while to see if he needed a ride to work but throughout his more than thirty-minute shower, I began to wonder if he was waiting for me to leave. So, I left, cursing myself in the car. I didn't want to leave, but I also didn't want him to fear that I was reading more into the preceding events than there actually was.

Fortunately, I was wrong. He had called me later that day and we progressively spent more and more time (mostly nights) together. We developed our own relationship that blossomed into more than each other could have ever hoped for.

As I walked along the cold pavement, I tried to keep my mind off of the chill. I was still trying to remember how I ended up wrapped in his arms in a flurry of romance the night before. It was all just a beautiful blur. But at that moment I was walking silently home alone. I had slipped out of his apartment before he could wake. I had left my new prince charming to return to my toad before anyone could ask any questions.

His proximity was of great convenience to our affair. To drive, one had to take a roundabout way on curvy hillside roads. His apartment was in one of the new developments outside of town. As the crow flies, however, one only needed to spend six minutes on the right footpath through the woods to arrive at the end of my street and then another five to arrive home. The footpath could be difficult in the dark, but I had grown up in those woods and knew the way by heart. I was careful to avoid sticker bushes that would tear at my clothes and legs and leave evidence, but the rocks and sticks underfoot were sometimes painful, but not unbearable. I was careful to try to be home before sunrise to avoid the judgmental eyes of my neighbors. In the summer, it had proved a slight challenge since the sun rose early and I did not want to leave my prince's bed. But, with the days growing shorter and the nights longer, we could extend our time together little by little.

I must admit, a part of me feels guilty about my adultery. But then, I was unhappy. Life is too short to be unhappy. It's not that I didn't love my toad. I did love him. But he was becoming more slovenly and lazy. I desperately needed those butterflies back. I needed to be needed. I needed love and excitement. Yes, it sounds self-centered. Should my toad find me out, his heart would be broken. But, what of my broken heart? What of my needs? I know my toad loved me but I *need* affection. Why not divorce? Why did I stay and sneak around? As I said, I loved him and his heart would shatter like glass. I couldn't bear the thought of causing him such pain. I am selfish, not heartless.

I walked up my driveway and turned onto the walkway that led around my house. All the windows were dark. Good, I thought, he's still asleep. I followed the walkway around the garden to the back of the house. I looked around carefully before I slipped down through the basement window as I had done when I was a child.

I had inherited my childhood home after my parents had passed away when a drunk driver collided with their car. My toad moved in shortly thereafter. We had been together for some years at that point and he was to help me with my bills for a short time. He promptly made himself at home. He moved things, disposed of items that had great sentimental value to me, and completely turned the house upside down. Every night after he came home, he would watch the television and down one beer after another, leaving the empty bottles for me to clean. He was well employed and so said he needed his relaxation time after a hard day at work. When I tried to express my unhappiness to him, he told me if I was that unhappy, I should just leave him. There was no middle ground. I wanted to try to work out our problems and talk to each other. For him, it was all or nothing.

He would tell me that our relationship was the most important thing to him. He had meant it once. But not anymore. I knew he still loved me. But when he said it, the emotion and tenderness in his eyes were gone. He wanted to spend time with me, but only if it was something that he wanted to do (usually sitting around the house). The long walks at the park and dinners at new restaurants, and games with friends that we had once seen as adventures together were now tedious. If I attempted to spend time with them without him, he would accuse me of talking about him behind his back. Steadily, our friends dropped away. I became isolated and my home began to feel like a prison. My one escape was work, where I could interact with like-minded people and feel like a human again. He didn't want to hear about work or my projects. He wanted dinner and sometimes to watch a show with me. That was all our relationship had boiled down to. I knew I still mattered to him. I just wasn't as important anymore.

Fortunately, the laundry room is in the basement. I pulled some less conspicuous clothing from the dryer, changed, and tiptoed up the stairs to the first floor. I strode into the living room quietly. My papers and computer were still set up on the coffee table. I heard the floorboards creak. I rushed to the couch and pretended to be asleep just as his feet touched the last step from upstairs. I could feel him walk up to me. He stood, looking down at me for quite some time. He smelled like dirty underwear and I tried not to wrinkle my nose. I felt a gentle touch on my shoulder and then a sharp squeeze. I slowly opened my eyes and pretended to yawn.

"Where have you been?" He stood over me.

"I must have fallen asleep while I was working on my project for work. The deadline is in two days."

He was silent for a moment. "I came down last night and you weren't here."

"I went for a walk pretty late. I couldn't sleep; worrying too much about this project, I guess."

"Oh."

That's all he could say? 'Oh.'

I suddenly felt as if he was calling my bluff.

He turned towards the kitchen. "Eggs?"

He knew I didn't eat eggs but I kept up the charade of politeness. "No thanks. I'm going to get a shower."

I was secretly hoping to wash off the deep cologne from my prince before he noticed it.

I walked upstairs and into the bathroom. I stripped down and held my long brunette hair to my nose. It smelled like my prince and me. The fruity aroma of my cheap shampoo clashed with his expensive cologne but the fact that it was our two scents together sent my mind back to that night. It had been a good night. I stepped over the lip of the tub and turned on the water. I daydreamed through my shower. I imagined my prince standing with me in the hot running water. I had my hands on his bare chest and looked up into his dark, chocolate eyes. His arms were wrapped around my torso, hands on my back. He pulled me in for a passionate kiss before lathering each other and playfully throwing foam. I only snapped back to reality once I realized the water had run cold.

I toweled off and strode into the bedroom. I walked up to my dresser and ran my fingers lightly over the box on top of it. I opened up my antique jewelry box. Inside was my grandmother's sapphire necklace. A blue heart was set in silver with a tear-drop-shaped pearl hanging from it- the crying heart. I related so much to the jewelry.

I picked it up carefully and gently ran my finger over the dark stone. She was wearing it the night she died. I was a lot like my grandmother and so we were quite close until her untimely death when I was twelve.

My grandfather was a sweet man and was taken from us far too early. Fearing loneliness, she remarried a wealthy retiree shortly after. He was a brute of a man. He kept my grandmother shut in the house and tried to force her away from the family. I hated him.

As I turned the stone over and over in my hand, I likened it to my grandmother and myself. Here was this beautiful heirloom meant for the world to see, but instead it was kept shut in a box, away from admiring eyes. My husband forced me into such a situation. I love him, I really do, but I thoroughly enjoy a social life.

I was always a social butterfly. I had many friends and loved spending time with them. Since high school, the vast majority of my friends had been men. People told me it was because I was beautiful. I just thought of myself as one of the guys. I didn't see what he was doing to me at first. In the beginning, he expressed distaste for one male friend who, shortly thereafter, stopped speaking to me. Then another and another started to fall away. Soon I had to report where I would be and when I would be there. He had to know who I was with if I was anywhere but work. Sometimes it became such a hassle to try to be with my friends that I just stayed in and sat on the couch, bored to the brink of insanity. I was the blue stone that was carved to be seen but kept locked away.

I carefully tucked the necklace back into the box and closed the lid tightly. I dressed and went down the stairs to the kitchen. He sat at the table in his boxer shorts, the elastic stretched to its limit and his belly lopped over his thighs. He shoveled piles of eggs and charred sticks of bacon into his mouth. I loved this disgusting creature. I was sure of it.

I walked up behind him and kissed the top of his head. He didn't look up. I poured myself a cup of coffee and leaned against the counter. I breathed in the rejuvenating aroma.

"I have to work today." He shoveled more eggs into his mouth.

It was Saturday but I wasn't surprised. He often worked weekends. I think that fact was one of the wedges that had been driven between us.

"When will you be home?"

"Late." He got up and put his plate in the sink. He never looked at me as he turned and headed up the stairs.

After he left, I went down to the basement to wash my clothes. Fruit and cologne. The mixture was intoxicating as I threw the garments into the washing machine. I suddenly felt very alone. My mind drifted back to my prince. I need those strong arms around me. I need that familiar face in my back between my shoulder blades with his breath heating me to the core. His hypnotic heartbeat was a lullaby. His love made me feel unworthy. I sighed yet again and went back upstairs.

I tried to call my best friend. She had introduced me to my prince and I wanted to go out with her while my husband was at work so we could talk.

Ring. Ring. Voicemail.

I was concerned that I hadn't been able to reach her recently. She hadn't shown up at work at the magazine for quite some time. She had a stalker at work whom she was very afraid of. Repeated attempts to report him to human resources had done nothing to deter him. I hoped he hadn't done anything to her.

I sat on the couch and stared at the ceiling. I was bored. I looked at my computer screen. My assignment was complete. It had been for some time. Thankfully, my husband was none-the-wiser. I closed the computer and cleaned up my notes. I piddled around the house for a while, cleaning dishes and wiping the stove from his mess. I switched around the laundry and carried my purse upstairs.

I fed the cat and dawdled around the kitchen a bit before returning to the couch. I lay down and stared at the ceiling again. I was tired. I hadn't gotten much sleep. I smiled as I thought of my prince. His broad chest and perfect arms created a flawless picture on the other side of my eyelids.

I heard a buzzing sound. I opened my eyes, annoyed that I was brought out of my daydream. It buzzed again. My cell phone, with barely a charge left, was vibrating across the coffee table. My prince! I rushed from the couch to answer my cell phone.

"Hello, Angel." I loved the sound of his voice. "You left this morning before I got a chance to say goodbye."

"I had to get back before he noticed."

"Would you care to meet me for lunch and give me another chance to say it?"

Butterflies! "I would love to."

"I will meet you at our spot at noon."

"Okay, my prince. See you there."

"See you soon, Angel."

I rushed up the stairs, almost tripping over the cat. I scoured my closet to find a luncheon outfit that would please my prince. I knew he didn't care what I wore but *I* cared. I selected a blue-gray sweater that gave just enough hint of cleavage to be seductive and blue jeans. I fussed over my long, wavy hair for almost an hour. It never looked just right. Makeup, perfume, and a silver Celtic knot pendant to complete the look; I was ready to leave. Twenty to twelve. I almost tripped over the cat again as I rushed out to my car.

Our spot was a tiny bookstore and cafe that sat on the river shore. It wasn't much, but it had great sandwiches and it was far enough from home that I was confident my husband would never find me there; not that he would ever be caught in a bookstore in the first place. It had a great atmosphere and we always sat at the same corner table overlooking the river.

He was standing on the steps to the door waiting for me. His hands were behind his back and a broad smile was spread over his face. He looked stunning in his ruby button-down shirt and black slacks. I loved it when he wore red. It was such a warm, inviting color.

"Hello." I smiled with feigned innocence.

He took his hand from behind his back. He had found my missing shoe.

I laughed, "Where was it? I looked everywhere."

"Apparently everywhere but the aquarium. It must have landed in there when you kicked it off. Don't worry, I dried it and removed as much of the fish smell as I could."

I pretended to be embarrassed. He smiled as he put his arm around me and led me inside. I breathed deeply as we walked in. I loved the familiar smells of the store. Freshly printed paper, coffee, and bread filled my nostrils. I loved it there.

We sat at our usual table and I looked out over the water. It was sunny out and the light danced on the water as if to its own tune. A few boats dotted docks along the shoreline.

"Be with me," he blurted out.

I snapped out of my trance and turned my head quickly to look at him. Did he just say what I think he did? He couldn't have.

"What did you say?" I think my expression was something of confusion or disbelief.

"I said 'be with me.'" He took my hand. "Leave your husband. He doesn't make you happy. I do. Leave him and come be with me."

I was in shock. I'm not sure how long I stared at him with my mouth gaped open. "I can't leave him. I love him."

"I know you do but you aren't in love with him anymore. And he doesn't respect you. I know it's not fair of me to ask you to do this but please at least think about it. We make each other so happy. You deserve to be happy. He obviously doesn't love you the way I do."

"I can't. He isn't a bad man. He just has other things that are more important right now."

"Nothing should be more important than you."

I couldn't believe this was happening. It was all so surreal. We went back and forth all through lunch. He kept reminding me how long I had been unhappy and I kept reminding him that it was only recently that things had started getting miserable in my house. We decided to continue our discussion walking across the bridge that spanned the river.

It was cold over the water. The autumn wind whipped at my hair and stung my cheeks. I held his arm tightly, attempting to keep warm. He continued to talk about what our life together could and should be. I suddenly became very annoyed. Of course, he could talk about how wonderful it will be and how easy it should be for me to leave my husband. He was single. There was no risk for him. I looked up at him. He continued to talk.

He said he understood that a divorce would be difficult. He promised to be there for me through it all. He would be my shoulder to cry on; my emotional rock! Our love would rival Antony and Cleopatra. I was unsure if his irony with that statement was intentional. Everything he said was candy to my ears. I could visualize this lie together. My heart wanted so much to be happy.

My heart was falling for all of this, but my head was not. Many of these words were ones had I heard before from my toad and I suspected the silver tongue with which he spoke was forked.

We stopped midway across the bridge. He looked into my eyes. "You are so beautiful. You should be mine."

With that statement, it all came together and I suddenly knew what he truly wanted. He didn't want to be with me. He wanted to own me. I was more of a trinket to him than I was to my husband. I swallowed the urge to break down and weep. This was my life. I was doomed to belong to someone, never to be with someone.

He walked me back to my car. He hugged me and kissed me passionately. He asked me to promise to think about what he had said. I promised but it felt hollow. I did think about what he said but not the way he intended me to.

The car ride home felt long and lonely. Maybe I wasn't meant to be happy. I was just a thing to both of them.

I pulled into the driveway and turned off the car. As I walked into the house, I looked around. It almost felt as if I was seeing everything for the first time. Here it was. This was our home. We had built this life together. It was our portrait on the wall. This was our furniture and our dishes. Yes, I had purchased it all, but it was ours. Sure, he had thrown away things that were important to me and he had isolated me from my friends and... My head began to hurt. I walked upstairs to lie down.

I kicked off my shoes and flopped on the bed. My eyes wandered to the jewelry box. I thought of the necklace inside with that beautiful blue stone. It was too great for how it was treated. My head was pounding harder as I thought of what my prince had said. He wanted me, not to be with me. My eyelids felt heavy.

It was dark when I awoke. My husband was standing over me naked, apparently fresh from the shower. My stomach felt a little uneasy as I looked at his gross physique. He had my car keys in one hand and an overnight bag in the other.

"Choose." His face was red and his eyes looked as if he had been crying.

"What are you talking about?" I slowly sat up; my head was still throbbing.

"Me or him. I'm tired of this game."

"What game?"

"I know you have been seeing someone else. You are my wife. I love you. But I can't keep pretending anymore."

It felt as if it had come from nowhere. Had he seen us at the bridge? I was almost relieved by the confrontation but how DARE he be mad at me? He was the one who had put me in such a situation. I'm not sure what came over me. I think I'd finally reached my breaking point. My toad had no affection for me. My price wanted to possess me. Why couldn't either of them just be in love with me? I stood and looked him in the eye.

"Why not?" As I confronted him, I felt tears move into my eyes. "You've been pretending nothing is wrong for the better part of our marriage. I've tried to talk to you. You blow me off or lie and say you'll try but you don't. You never keep your promises to me. You don't even want to be around me anymore. I'm just another knick-knack on the shelf. It only becomes a problem when I find someone else who makes me happy?"

He looked stunned for a moment, then spoke softly. "I thought if I ignored the problem, it would go away. It took realizing that I can lose you to open my eyes."

"You should have thought about that all the times I have been trying to talk to you about it." I threw my hands in the air. "But no. You pushed it aside, just like you did me. Why do you want to keep me? I'm just a thing to you. You don't want to be with me, you just want to be able to say I am yours. You don't know what love even is! You can call me selfish all you want but you're who's selfish. You don't care about my happiness. You don't even care about *us*. You admit you ignored the problems and hoped they would go away. Well, guess what; you ignored me, so you can't be mad that I'm going away!"

The more I screamed, the redder his face became. I knew he had a temper. I knew I should have stopped, but I just kept yelling. His hand came back. My cheek stung as I fell backward, his fist pulling back for another blow. His eyes suddenly softened. He realized what he had just done. He grabbed a pair of pants from the floor and slammed the door as he stormed out of the room. He had hit me. I never thought he would do it.

I lay back on the bed. The tears that had made their way to the surface were now stinging my eyes. I didn't even know I had any tears left. In all the fights we had had, never once had he laid a hand on me. I was alone in the world. I loved two men who didn't love me. How did my life end up like this? Why didn't the Powers that Be think I deserved to be happy? Through the blurry film of tears, my eyes fell on my grandmother's jewelry box. She had had a similar problem. She, unlike me, had found freedom. I imagined my grandmother's face. I thought of the misery her second husband had put her through. I was not going to be her. I wiped away my tears, walked over to the jewelry box, and pulled out the sapphire. It was meant to be seen and loved. So was I. I put it around my neck. I looked back at the box. I clicked a latch that opened a secret compartment. I had seen my grandmother do it the night she died. Inside was an old steel dagger. Its handle was silver and in the hilt was mounted a blue sapphire, identical to the one around my neck. They were a set; a reminder and a solution passed down from wife to wife in my family. It was the only true solution.

I opened the bedroom door quietly. I walked down the stairs and turned the corner at the bottom. My toad was a lump on the couch. I walked up behind him and kissed the top of his head. I hugged him around the neck. My arm felt warm as my sweater was soaked through with blood. He tried to turn to look at me. He bubbled a little blood from his mouth and slumped over quietly.

I breathed a sigh of relief as I walked down to the basement to change. I put my sweater in the washer. I used the stream of water to wash off my arm. I dried off and pulled on a bright blue blouse from the dryer. As I walked back upstairs, I could hear my cell phone ring. I pulled it from my purse.

"Hello, Angel. How are you feeling?"

"I'm much better now." I was surprised by the calm in my voice given what I had just done.

"Good, would you like to come to my place for a bit after your husband falls asleep? I think we should talk some more and I need to see you."

I was angered a little but leveled my voice. "No need to wait. He won't be a problem now."

"Oh. Okay then. I guess you thought about what I said. I'll see you soon then."

"I did think about it. I'll see you soon." He sounded thrilled.

I hung up the phone. Yes, I did think about what you said. There's only one option for me now.

Apartment 3C. I had been here time and

again. I walked in and threw my coat on the couch.

"Hello?" I called.

"I'm in the bedroom."

I walked back to the farthest room in the apartment. He lay in the bed. There were candles lit on the dresser and windowsill and two champagne flutes sat on the nightstand.

"What's all this for?" I looked at the romantic display.

"I thought we should celebrate our new life together."

I climbed on top of him. He smiled. His beautiful eyes crinkled as he lay back on the pillows. I ran my hand down his chest and over his heart.

"I'm sorry, my Darling Prince, but there will be no life together."

The sharp blade slid through his ribcage easily. He had broken my heart. I had pierced his. He gasped and tried to sit up but fell back, clutching his chest with one hand and reaching for me with the other. His blood stained the azure silk sheets we had laid on so many times before. He gradually stopped moving and the life left his sky-colored eyes. I felt as if a great weight had been lifted from my shoulders but my heart hurt. I took a sip of champagne as I dismounted his body. I looked at myself in his mirrored closet doors.

This is where I stand. I see my reflection now. My blouse matches the stone I wear perfectly. I feel as if we are one. We are free. But to what end? We are here for all to see, yet now alone. What of the next man I am to meet? He will want to own me too. That's all they ever want of me.

I look at the blood-covered blade. This is my solution. I drain my champagne flute before setting it on the dresser. I lay down next to my prince. His body is still warm as I caress his arm. I close my eyes one last time and see my husband's face as the blade passes through my ribs and into the very part of me that is broken. It doesn't hurt now and I feel cold. I turn my head to gaze one last time at my prince. I had thought he was going to be different.

Blue- unhappy, desolate, downcast; one color with so much meaning. I am truly blue.

~ 6 ~

INDIGO

I love this time of night- just as dusk is settling in and the sky is a splendor of indigo that fades to black. High in the violet hills that surround my little town, all manner of day creature lullabies its little ones to sleep. Meanwhile, creatures of the night scatter to find breakfast. There is nothing more peaceful than this simplistic bliss. It is my one escape.

I stop at a corner, a mere two blocks from my house. This is where it had happened.

* * * * *

It was a warm summer night. Peaceful solitude surrounded me. I was returning from a walk in the hills. The scent of warm violets was intoxicating and irresistible. This had become my evening routine ever since the insomnia had set in.

I was tired of it all. I was tired of the work. I was tired of the stress. I was tired of being tired. My entire world was constantly in a fog. Things around me felt so surreal I often wondered if I was not, in fact, dreaming. I couldn't remember the last truly deep slumber I had fallen into. I longed for that rush of total, blissful, peace. I deeply desired its warm embrace to overcome my body. My limbs would grow limp, my eyes heavy, and my head would weigh down until it was abruptly stopped by the keyboard at my desk. Alas, I woke to a dream-like state of utter exhaustion.

This was not the life I had planned for myself. I was beautiful. I knew it as well as everyone around me. I was what every woman wanted to be. I had long legs, blonde hair, blue eyes, and flawless skin. I was busty even as a pre-teen and Marylin Monroe had nothing on my figure. I had started modeling at three years old and moved up quickly. I was going to be a woman of the world. My looks were going to carry me to exotic beaches in faraway lands. They would beckon to me to model amongst the golden and white sands. I had a life of luxury at my fingertips. I was going to use my fame to further create my own brand. I would design gowns o shimmering silk, the finest lace, and beautiful stones to adorn the elite.

I married my first photographer straight out of high school. I was young and easily smitten. He was rapidly making a name for himself and it seemed like a perfect move to hasten both of our careers. Everything was falling into place before the accident.

It wasn't even raining that night. We were driving along a winding, dark road on the way home from dinner at a friend's cabin. We were happy and laughing and commenting on our host's deplorable interior decorating. We blinked and the buck was directly in front of the car. My husband reflexively swerved and the car rolled. When I woke up, I was in the hospital. I was bandaged and in pain. My flawless face had been shredded by broken glass. The right side of my body was mangled. My nose was broken and I had facial burns from the airbag. The passenger side of the car had hit a tree. My husband escaped with only minor injuries.

Nothing was the same after that. The reconstructive surgeries could not completely restore my face. The physical therapy could not make me graceful again. My husband had affair after affair. He finally admitted he had planned on riding my celebrity. He said he never loved me and we divorced.

I was supposed to follow my dreams. My vision was never to sit in a drab and dreary office day in and day out. I never wanted to take orders from a boorish woman who fancied herself a god of the industry. I was supposed to have my own business- nothing large. I would sit in my office with my dog at my heels. I was supposed to make beautiful gowns of shimmering silk and lace. Each one would be a work of art. I would model them and sell them, eking out a meager but comfortable living. That was my fantasy. I often daydreamed of such things. Then my eyes would open and I would be face to face with a computer screen filled with e-mails and diagrams. In what dark alley had I turned left instead of right? Why was I here, miserable and lost amongst the crowd?

I often asked such questions though I had known the answer. I had bet it all on my beauty. Instead of attending design school, I had jumped straight into my modeling career. I didn't need college just yet; there was plenty of time and I needed to create my brand—my name—first. The accident had taken that all away. After the divorce, the insomnia set in. I had been forced to take a job at a small magazine to survive. All of the money in our joint account had been mine. I burned through most of it on medical bills and divorce attorney fees. Though I won alimony, it was pennies. So here I sat, day after day, looking at pictures of women who were living my dream. Their beauty was flawless. Their smiles were perfect. I didn't even smile anymore. As I selected which of their images were worthy of being in the magazine, I wondered if they knew how easily it could all be taken from them.

Each night I would go home to an empty house. My dog was my only companion. My family and most of my friends had stopped talking to me when I called them out over their jealousy of my now-gone beauty. I had no one. The male admirers who had once flocked to me now grimaced in disgust. I once stood out, shining above all around me. Everyone wanted to be near me. Everyone loved me. I had male admirers even after I had married. Life was great. As my husband and admirers faded from my life, so did my ability to sleep.

I often found myself whittling away at the insomnia-plagued nights by taking long walks through the flowers outside of town. There was a myth one could hear the ghosts of children's laughter in those hills. I think part of me wished it was true. I wanted so much to know there was someone else there; someone who would see past the scars. Instead, there was only my dog and me.

After the divorce, I retreated to a little house in a newer development that I had found in a small town that sat in a violet-covered valley. It was close to the city so I could drive myself to the doctor's appointments and when I was well enough to, find work. But it was secluded enough that I didn't feel the world staring at my disfigurement. It was just my dog and me and he didn't care how I looked.

One warm evening in late spring, the sun had long set, and my dog and I set off on what would likely be the first of several walks as the night wore on without sleep. I carried a large, heavy flashlight to guide our way even though we walked the same roads every night. As I rounded a corner, I saw a man I had never met before. He wore a dark baggy shirt and old dark pants. His clothes were dirty and well-worn. He had shaggy black hair and a slight beard. I could make out distinctly well-defined musculature beyond the baggy clothes. I found him oddly attractive beneath such an unkempt appearance.

As he stood near the lamppost, he looked up at me. His eyes were dark and sullen. He was a vagabond. Drifters often found themselves in the violet hills. Every summer they found temporary work harvesting wild honey and selling the beautiful blooms. The hills were warm, peaceful, and irresistible.

He watched me carefully as my dog and I passed. His body remained motionless but his eyes never left me.

When I came home, I could still feel his eyes on me. I looked carefully to make sure I hadn't been followed before closing the door. I fixed myself a mug of warm milk and shook two sleeping pills from a bottle. I stared at the tiny blue tablets in my palm. I didn't know why I was bothering to take them. Even on the rare occasion that they did help me sleep it was never the restful, rejuvenating tranquility, I yearned for. I generally spent what little sleep I did get writhing from unknown nightmares or I would find myself constantly waking. I shrugged my shoulders, popped the pills in my mouth, and washed them down with the warm milk.

Such was my routine. I tucked my dog in at the foot of the bed before pulling my covers up under my chin. I lay with my eyes open, staring at the ceiling, waiting for the drugs and warm milk to take effect. The clock ticked, my dog snored, and the wind rushed by my window. I had all the ingredients for a perfect night's rest. Sadly, it was not to be.

That night I lay staring at the ceiling, waiting for the drugs to decide if they were going to take effect. I thought about the vagabond. Perhaps it had been desire that I'd seen in those eyes. It had been so long that a man had looked at me lustfully. Would I even recognize such a look? He was ruggedly handsome in a dirt-covered, homeless, possibly deranged sort of way.

The next day at work the entire office was buzzing. There was a killer on the loose. A young woman's corpse had been found rotting inside a man's home and he was nowhere to be found. Everyone was commenting on how strange it was that the woman was tucked in bed with delicate care. Necrophile and other such unpleasant words were thrown around haphazardly.

I thought about what it would be like to kill someone. The energy that must go through a murderer's body must be invigorating and intoxicating. Adrenaline courses through your veins with every strike of your knife or explosion from your gun. A drug. I found myself wishing I had the courage to perform such an action. Maybe then I would stop feeling so numb to the world.

The day was a slow-motion blur. Sadly, and fortunately, I had become accustomed to functioning with this inability to focus. When the clock struck five, I dragged myself home.

After dinner, I harnessed my dog, grabbed the flashlight, and we went out for our walk in the hills. A soft, indigo sky draped over us. Absolute beauty. My husband and I had often taken similar paths to these when we were dating. We lived in the city but would slip away to seclusion whenever we could. Our relationship was frowned upon by many of my friends and family. I was still in high school, after all, and he was in his twenties in a budding career. I didn't care. He always had a way of making me feel more special than anyone else. He often told me that my beauty was the only thing that could dwarf that of the amethyst sky above us. I missed him deeply. Sometimes. Then I would remember that my attractiveness was the only thing about me he had ever loved. While I had seen his career as a stepping stone for my own, I did at least have some affection for him. It was not reciprocated. It had all been an act. That made me truly bitter.

Again, the vagrant was at the same corner. He watched me pass with the same dark eyes.

I nodded my head toward him as a gesture of courtesy, but he did not respond in kind. I don't know why I had wanted some kind of acknowledgment, but it upset me that I didn't receive one.

Same routine. Home. Warm milk and sleeping pills. I lay in bed with my dog at my heels. She snored loudly as the clock ticked. I thought about my husband. This insomnia had started when he told me he could no longer see me as beautiful and no one else would either. That was four years to the day before my first sighting of the drifter. Four years of no sleep. Eight months without my husband's arms. Loneliness accompanied the numbness I felt toward the world.

We used to dance on our balcony in the city while watching the indigo sky fade to speckled black. He would tell me how much he loved me and how he couldn't imagine being without me. We used to smile and sip wine and talk about the future. I used to be able to feel his arms around me just by looking at that sky. I longed to feel so desired again. I had once been desired by every man who knew me, but it was all lost.

It was another long night. It was not at all restful, but at least it was something.

The next morning, my friend and coworker came and sat at my desk. He was a staff editor I had met as a teenager. He had helped me get this job. After my husband left, he had a position available and while I loathed the work, I was grateful for his help. We had once been flirtatious and toyed with the idea of being lovers years ago. I had once toyed with the hope that he would consider rekindling our tryst but he hardly spoke to me after the insomnia set in.

"I'm worried about you," he said as he put his hand on my shoulder.

"Why?"

"You have lost an awful lot of weight. You look like you haven't slept in months. Have you seen a doctor?"

I decided to throw caution to the wind. I smiled. "Maybe you could come over tonight and we could talk about it." I gently ran my fingertips over his knee.

"Honey, I know what we used to have but that was another life. I like you and all but, no. You look like death warmed over. I wouldn't dream of sleeping with you. Just get yourself some help." He left my cubicle.

He rejected me. The only human companion I had. Death warmed over? I couldn't look that bad. I went to the restroom and looked in the mirror. I had lost a little weight. My eyes were darker and my skin was pale. I didn't think I looked quite as bad as death. It was the scars that were reminiscent of a corpse. The surgeons did the best they could. People told me they couldn't even see them, but they were just being kind. I was Frankenstein's monster.

Same routine. Home. Dinner. Walk the dog. I kept thinking about what my friend had said. Death warmed over. I had lost my beauty. I had lost the one thing that had made me so desirable. Now I was alone. I was going to be alone forever.

I closed my eyes and called out to the indigo sky. "Bring me the same peace and comfort you used to! Please!"

I opened my eyes. The vagabond stood at the corner. The same dark, somber eyes watched me. I walked up to him, tears in my own eyes.

"You think I'm beautiful, don't you?" I held

my arms apart so he could get a good look at me.

He turned to walk away from me.

"Look at me! Don't you want me?"

I grabbed his arm and tried to pull him to face me, but he was stronger. He ripped his arm away. I'm not sure what happened. That electrified feeling I had daydreamt about seemed to come to fruition. I was angry. I was hurt. I was frantic. I was every emotion I had superseded all at once. I had the heavy metal flashlight in my right hand. I pulled it back and cracked it into his temple as he tried to walk away again. He fell to the ground.

I looked at his body. It was the first time I had felt anything real in years. I looked up at the indigo sky. The pale purple was like a comforting blanket, just as it had been years ago. I crawled into the bed under its warmth and slept- truly slept- for the first time.

The next day at work my friend came into my cubicle. "You look great today!"

"Thanks." I smiled.

"Did you go to the doctor?"

"Nope. Just tried something new."

"Well keep it up!" He slapped the top of the cubicle wall as he walked away.

"I think I will."

~ 7 ~

VIOLET

Violet is a pure color. To taint it with any other makes an entirely new color. Because of its purity, it is a color that can evoke a wide range of emotions in people. I had never really thought about it very deeply until my only daughter was stolen from me. After her death, I had an entirely new realization and appreciation for it. For me, it is a color that evokes feelings of both love and hate.

It was difficult for my wife and me to conceive a child. We had tried for years after we were married. We tried everything we saw in a book or on television. Nothing ever seemed to work. We had seen several doctors and were told to just keep trying as fertility treatments were far outside of our budget. Finally, all of our efforts paid off. I came home from work one day and my wife jumped into my arms. She was crying and laughing at the same time. I will never forget how happy she looked as she sobbed and told me the good news. This was our dream come true. We lay in bed awake all night telling each other it could be a false positive and not to get our hopes up at the same time we talked about names, making our own baby food versus buying it, where we would put the crib, and how to decorate the nursery.

A few days later, she confirmed the positive result at the doctor's office. We couldn't contain our excitement. We called all of our family and friends that night. That weekend, we drove into the city and began buying everything in sight. By the time we arrived back home, our car was laden with shopping bags filled with books, baby clothes, bottles, and everything else we could find. It may have been a little premature for us to do so, but we were just too happy.

While she was at work the next day, I cleared

out my study. I painted the walls a pale shade of purple, my wife's favorite color. My neighbor came over and helped me put together the crib and hang new curtains. By the time she came home, the entire nursery was perfect. When she walked in and saw what I had done, she burst into tears and hugged me so tightly I almost couldn't breathe.

The next seven and a half months were full of anticipation and excitement. Our dreams were finally coming true. We didn't know how quickly those dreams would become a nightmare. One night, my wife walked into the living room where I sat watching television. She said she didn't feel well. I looked at her. She was pale, her eyes were sunken, and she looked faint. I shoved her into the car and rushed her to the hospital.

At first, they didn't seem to want to help her. I begged for them to do something, but my pleas were met with repeated calls to calm down. When she slumped over in a wheelchair, they realized I was not exaggerating. They took her into an emergency room and called for several doctors. I'll never forget the way she looked when they ripped her away from me. Her lips were blue and her eyes were gone. A hospital waiting room is a terrible place. There is no comfort in being surrounded by people as anxious as you are, the ill, and the injured. The worst are the children. They play in a corner with donated toys, oblivious to the horrors around them. I tried to sit, but I couldn't stay still. I paced even though my legs felt weak. It was a long night. I was scared. What if something had happened to her or even the baby? My mind began to reel with thoughts of losing either of them. They terrified me. I tried to focus on other things. I tried to watch the television and I played with the fish in the tank in the waiting room. I walked back and forth from the vending machine to my chair, never buying anything to eat. I was too tense to eat.

When I saw a doctor I recognized come out I immediately knew something was wrong. He said he wasn't sure what happened. My wife had started to hemorrhage internally. It was a placental bleed that they couldn't stop. They couldn't save her. I collapsed to the floor. This wasn't real. This couldn't be happening to me.

The doctor knelt beside me and put his hand on my shoulder. He asked me if I would like to meet my daughter. Through my tears, I looked up at him in disbelief. I had a daughter. They had managed to save her.

As I held her in my arms, I promised to take the best care of her. She was all that mattered in my world. I would be the best father ever and she would know that her mother had wanted nothing more than to meet her. I kissed my Violet on her sleeping head as I made my vow.

I spoiled my daughter. I knew I did. In my mind, it was justified. I had to take the role of both parents and so doted on her a little more. I was determined to keep my word. She truly was all that mattered.

Then, one night when she was five years old, she crept into my bed and shook my shoulder.

"What's wrong?" I asked drowsily.

"Daddy, I don't feel good."

My mind immediately went back to my wife. I bolted from my bed and threw on a shirt over my pajama pants. She was never a sick child. I grabbed her, still in her nightgown, and rushed to the hospital again.

Once more I paced in the lobby of the hospital. Once more I waited, frightening myself with thoughts of what was wrong with my baby. I couldn't lose her too.

My stomach lurched when I saw the doctor. Violet was anemic and it didn't look good. The doctor told me I could lose her. The thought virtually shredded the fabric of my being.

I came to the hospital every day. She was always happy to see me. Though she looked dreadful, she never seemed afraid of what was happening to her. Every day she grew paler and paler. For months, her suffering dragged on. I watched my baby slowly fade away. Leukemia is a terrible thing to watch a child die from. The transfusions and transplants weren't enough. There were bigger hospitals and other treatments, but with no access to insurance and no income, they were far out of reach.

I was a broken man, grief-stricken, and essentially destroyed. My sweetest Violet had died at the hands of merciless bureaucrats. Not long after she had gotten sick, it was deemed that I was causing too much trouble for the company by trying to care for her and so my employment was abruptly terminated. It was as if the last thirteen years of servitude had meant nothing. With no healthcare and no income, I was forced to watch my baby waste away.

They didn't care. The company that "treats its employees like family" had cast me aside. For what? Because I spent more time at the hospital than in the office. Because my little girl was scared and didn't want to be alone. Because I used all of my vacation and sick hours and was missing work unpaid. Because time and time again I was told the treatments had failed and she would not be coming home. Because I loved my daughter, they took her from me.

She was buried beside her mother and I spread freshly picked violet flowers over her grave. Standing alone in the rain with the two greatest loves in my life six feet below the earth in front of me, I swore that justice would be served. With no money for a lawyer, the courts refused to hear my desperate pleas for retribution. I wanted those murderers I had once called "friend" to feel my pain.

My wife's family and my own tried to console me. They claimed to feel my pain, but they had no idea how broken I was. I slipped into my own world. I hardly ever left home. I was always tired. To this day my thoughts are choppy and often incomplete. My mind was constantly reeling with some fantasy of vengeance. The more I thought about it, the more I realized that vengeance is a satisfying act. It is a gift to those who are being avenged. Whether it is oneself or a loved one, it is the greatest gift one can give.

They had killed her. My sweet baby girl. They had all killed her. They banished her flowing brown curls and wide green eyes from this earth forever. How could they do it? I loved her. She was my little violet angel. Born to my late wife six years ago, and they killed her. She was all I had left in the world. They stripped me of my living spirit, my little Violet. Those murderers had to be punished.

How? How could I punish these people? They were my neighbors and formerly my friends. I had been foolish enough to believe that once. I thought these people had cared for my family and me. No. They only cared about money. The more I brooded over their treachery, the angrier I became. If they could kill a child, the purest stage of human life, without remorse, then why couldn't I?

Months went by. I visited my darling's grave every night before bed. I loved to take her old books up into the hills where she lay and read her a bedtime story. The rolling flowers and sweet scent of their perfume were a comfort. Their color put my mind at ease and often brought a smile to my face. It was my wife's favorite color.

Late one night, I was walking home after saying goodnight to my baby and her mother. I heard a little giggle and a boy jumped out from behind a tree. He was a stout little thing no more than eight or nine years old. His blonde hair was cropped short. His blue eyes were partially hidden by chubby pink cheeks. I recognized him right away. He was the son of my former manager. I had seen him at the company picnic the year or two before. I asked him what he was doing out in the woods by himself.

"I am waiting for the ghost," he replied.

"What ghost would that be?"

"My dad says there is a little girl buried in

the flowers on this hill. The ghost of her daddy is up here every night."

It didn't take much to realize the boy's father was talking about me. "Why are you waiting for him?" I asked.

"I want to ask him why he is here."

"What do you mean?"

"My dad says he could live again if he would forget about her. I want to know why he doesn't just move on and live again. Doesn't he want to live?"

Forget about her? How can one forget their only daughter? That is as if to ask me to forget that I ever breathed or that my heart had ever beat! Forget about her? I fought tears of anger and heartache. I had once been alive. Your father helped kill me... helped kill her.

I tried to steady myself. "You should not be out so late by yourself." I put my arm across the boy's shoulders. "I will keep you company."

The next morning, I learned that my neighbor and former superior at work had lost something. His son. They found hardly a trace of the boy. Only a few drops of blood on his front doorstep and a purple flower petal beside the tiny crimson bubbles. His parents were devastated. I saw their tears on the television screen as they begged for any information to help find their little boy.

The police were dumbfounded. We lived in a town of sage violets. Everywhere you turned the precious flowers bloomed gloriously. Just outside of town, acres and acres of blossoms covered the landscape as far as the eye could see. It was not uncommon for petals or flowers to be tracked into homes. They were everywhere. My dearest wife loved it here. That is how my Violet had gotten her name.

Another week passed and another one of the sinners, an old enemy of my family who lived on the other side of town, lost one of their children. Again a few drops of blood and violet petals were all that were found of the child.

These strange disappearances were big news. Nothing like this had happened since the strange and brutal murder-suicide several months before. All the people feared for their children's lives. Once the parks were full of joy and screams of delight. The children had danced like shameless nymphs. They were frolicking and giggling;

wallowing in their youth and frivolity. It was an unabashed display of flesh amongst the purity of nature. There was no happier sight. But soon, the parks were bare and lifeless. Swings blew in the breeze and raccoons took up residence in the playhouses. After the children had started going missing, any and all youths in the entire town were no longer allowed to walk home from school or to be on the street without a guardian.

By the end of the month, five children had disappeared altogether. All that was found of each of them were a few drops of blood and the violet flower petals. Where were they going? No one knew. No one but me that is. Rumors and theories circled amongst the educated and the non-alike. What horrible person could hurt a child? They were all ignorant. They didn't know. If they would have looked harder, they would have known. But they were blind. I wasn't a person anymore. I was a ghost.

One night, I went to go read to my little angel in the hills that bore her name. It was a warm spring night. The moon was high in the dark purple sky accompanied by the twinkling lights of the stars. Crickets chirped contentedly and lightning bugs flickered in empty air. It was a peaceful walk. I felt a sense of contentment and safety, as if my family's spirits were all around me, watching me from behind the violet blooms. I knelt in the flowers that were so tall, it was near impossible to see me.

Hidden amongst the flowers was my darling Violet. A lifelike cement figurine of her depicted her asleep. Her mother lay next to her. My family. A few tears crept their way into my eyes. I looked around the ground at the offerings I had presented to them. I felt that they were happy with my work and almost satisfied with the gifts.

After a few silent and respectful moments, I heard a rustle in the flowers behind me. I turned and saw a familiar figure. It was my Violet's best friend; a neighbor girl who often came to our house for cookies and juice on sunny afternoons. My violet was very fond of her and I must admit, I thought of her as one of my own from time to time. It was her parents who enraged me most of all. It was her father who had signed my termination and my daughter's death warrant. It was her mother who threatened to call the police when I confronted him after Violet's death.

She asked what I was doing out so far from home so late at night. I told her I had come to say goodnight to my little girl. I asked her what she was doing out so late all alone. She said she had seen me leave my house and wanted to make sure I was all right.

I told her I was fine and that I was only there for a little while. I picked her up and started to carry her toward town. As she held onto my neck and looked over my shoulder, she let out a terrible gasp and pushed me away. We both fell to the ground. I played dumb and asked her what was wrong.

She pointed to the spot where I had been kneeling and screamed the most shrill note that had ever pierced my ears. I knew where she was pointing without even so much as a glance in that direction. There laid the bodies of the five missing children. Gifts for my darling Violet angel. Vengeance was the greatest gift one can give.

She said she was going to tell her daddy

and the families so they wouldn't have to worry anymore. I couldn't let her do that. Not after all the hard work I had gone through to make sure the murderers of my Violet suffer. They were gifts for my baby girl and I couldn't let anything get in my way.

The girl began to run towards town. I frantically looked around for a weapon or at least something to slow her down with. All there was in sight were those ever-tall blooms. I ripped a few out by their roots and ran after the girl. I tackled her and wrapped the stalks tightly around her neck. The girl tried to scream but the stems had cut off her vocal ability. A single tear rolled down her cheek as my dear sweet Violet's best friend fell limp and into a never-ending slumber. I watched her face slowly turn the color of the flowers and her eyes glazed over.

It reminded me of all the other children. I could feel their lives escaping their bodies. It was a cold yet gratifying feeling. They had to pay the price for their parents' cruel-hearted actions. I hated to do this. I loved children. I really did. But my Violet had to be avenged. I hadn't intended to kill her yet. I had wanted her parents to suffer most of all. I had wanted them to live in fear just a bit longer before I took her away from them. But what was done was done.

I dragged her body to where the others were. She took her place in the row of children. She lay still, silent as the night sky. Her hands were folded over her breast. Her face was at peace; forever to rest in solitude amongst the flowers.

The next morning the girl's family found their darling child missing and a few purple petals on their doorstep. I saw the barrage of police cars whirring down our otherwise quiet street and coming to a halt in front of their house. I could hear the sobs of the family and it brought a smile to my face. The police came to my door and I invited them in for tea. They declined and asked if I had known the girl. I said yes. They asked if I had seen her. I said not since the previous day. They asked if I had seen any suspicious people or vehicles and I said no. They thanked me for my time and left.

I stood amongst the flowers that night, looking at the peaceful bodies that lay beside my family. I knew it would only be a matter of time before they realized I had left blood because their children's blood was on their hands. They would eventually realize that Violet's was too and I wanted them to hear her name every time they spoke of their missing children. The petals I left them would see to that. Those petals would lead search parties that had already set out to this very spot and I didn't care. My work was complete. The children were dead, but I knew their spirits took comfort in that they died for a just cause. The murderous families that had killed my precious daughter paid dearly for what they had done.

Forever burned into their memories would be the name Violet.

~ 8 ~

INTERMISSION: HOW IT BEGAN

I feel myself falling. I'm not always tumbling down a rabbit hole like Alice or free-falling from a cliff like the coyote, but I am always falling. Everything is passing me like a blur. It's as if my days aren't really happening. I'm just watching them happen as I pass through them on the way to... the bottom? The ground? I don't know what exactly I am plummeting toward but I don't do it at a consistent speed. Sometimes I am falling slowly. I'm gently wafting through my day like a leaf in October. Things are passing by so calmly that I am able to reach out and touch them. Sometimes I can even move them and make things better. Some days I am tumbling. I fall a little and smack into something like a deadline and then I tumble some more and bump into a luncheon I had forgotten. On other days I am plunging through the world so fast that I can't actually see what is going on. I have no control or ability to slow my descent. These days are becoming more frequent. It's as if I roll out of bed and fall off of a cloud and go hurtling towards the earth below, and just when I think there might be a chance for me to grab a hold of something, it's time to go to bed, pretend to sleep, and start the next day.

Once a week I force myself down to the city. On Monday mornings I take my son to daycare to play while I head to the newspaper. It would be cheaper and easier to let him spend the day with my sister but I can't bring myself to leave him there. He wouldn't be in danger; we'll call it my ego. I kiss his head and tell him to be a good boy. He hugs me tightly and tells me he wants chicken fingers for lunch when I come to pick him up. I promise him a feast from our favorite in-and-out joint.

I had been forced to call in a few favors when I realized Iris had forsaken me. There were still trickles of money coming in from my books, but it wasn't enough to supplement my husband's income to care for four people. Thankfully, I have friends in good places. They took me on as a freelance writer. I write about whatever I'm told to but never anything I have a passion for. It's elegiac, but it's income.

At the office, the atmosphere is tense. There are whispers that the newspaper is losing too much money. Historically, the hills made internet in the valley and beyond almost impossible. Our community was somewhat stuck behind the times and we liked it that way. People relied heavily on the newspaper to find out what happened not only in town but further out in the city and even the world. Now, with the interlopers moving in, the internet is in much higher demand and therefore has become more easily accessible to all of us. Outsiders don't care for our "simple" ways. Because of this, we are putting more focus on our internet base as sales of paper dwindle. The printers fear for their jobs if the paper goes to an entirely electronic medium. There is also a rumor that a magazine from the city nearby wants to buy our small operation. Writers like me should be safe either way but I worry about my friends. We aren't close, but they are good people and I don't want to see anything bad befall them.

Monday mornings are our "roundtable" where those of us who don't report the immediate news discuss our projects. It is a nonsensical conversation that is more useful for eating hours of the day than actually accomplishing anything. The gossip columnist reports who has the most enviable whatever. The investigative journalist want-to-be catches us up on the latest mutilated pets of the newly arrived development inhabitants. The relationship advisor dishes on who is failing and who is cheating-anonymity only being maintained in print.

Then there's the fashionista. I catch her eye as she sits across from me. She's smiling again. She's always smiling and showing off those unnaturally white teeth and little wrinkles around her eyes. What does she have to be so damn happy about all the time? I have a deep-seated loathing for her. Does she feel pain? Does she feel sadness? She's always so happy. No one is naturally this happy. She must be heavily medicated- unnaturally happy to go with her unnatural teeth.

Her attempt at physical beauty is admirable, yet far from triumphant. Her lips are swollen cherries. Her cheeks are wilted plumbs. Her hair cascades like waves of wheat and chestnut as well as a few unidentifiable colors. It must have taken hours to paint and bleach this piece of art, yet, through it all, her devoid soul shines through, creating a scene of deep hideous disdain and self-loathing.

She knows something. I can see it in her cocky eyes. Her lips are pressed to keep the secret from escaping. Her look is not one of pity. It looks more like comeuppance. The secret she knows will lead to me getting what she feels I deserve. What? What are you hiding? Are you reveling in my failure? No. That's not a secret. What do you want?

She has hated me since my wedding day. She and my husband had been high school lovers (sweethearts is romanticizing it a bit) and she had been convinced that they were destined to be together while he saw her as a pretty bit of arm candy. She was angry when he had joined the ROTC and ended their relationship. Years later, she turned up at a newspaper in a small town that she has no roots (or friends) in. I personally believe she has followed him here.

I truly want to confront her one day (ideally with the front of my car) but I behave. There is too much tension here for me to do anything to risk losing my job...or going to prison.

A stranger comes into the front lobby. Our offices being small, we can all see him from the meeting room. He clearly wants to be sure we all have a good look at him and is careful to strike an impressive pose when he enters. Such pomp. Such arrogance. He holds his chest out and gazes ahead. He sees only what he wants to see. He has his followers and those who do not follow him need to be saved. His belly, fat from the spoils of others' patronage and servitude, presses haughtily at the buttons of his coat. The strain of movement could cause one to burst at any moment. He pulls the brim of his hat low over his brow to further the severity of his gaze rather than removing it indoors like a gentleman. He clutches a thick walking stick. He does not need the aid to walk but clearly revels in the sense of power each step gives him as it thuds on the floorboards, commanding respect. I subtly look at his feet. His shoes are slightly elevated so that he may further tower over those he views as enemies and followers.

This is the man we all fear. He wants to buy the paper and increase his number of followers by turning it into a subsidiary of his magazine from the city. He's going to save us all by making sure that we have a place in his growing media empire. Such a disgusting human being. The only thing that could make me sicker is if he asks me to start a blog- the gutter slime of styles of prose.

I look over at my editor. He looks very curious and confused. He is a wonderful person to work for but unfortunately, he is a weak man at heart. His receding hairline frames a lumpy but domed forehead. It is slightly bunched into creases by raised eyebrows. The marble white of his eyes is clearly visible as the orbs slightly bulge from their housing. His flat cheekbones and sagging jawline make his personal weakness into something visual. His nose, slightly crooked, hangs high over a mouth that is parted in preparation to ask a question.

I slide a sideways glance at the fashionista. Her smile has broadened. She knew he was coming. That deceitful little traitor had probably sought him out and secured herself a comfy position under the new regime. I keep finding new reasons to hate this woman.

With the arrival of our guest, our meeting is adjourned early. Fashionista carefully fixes her skirt as she stands and gives a little wave to the guest. As she walks past me, her look says a million words. She hates me as much as I hate her. She hasn't only secured a comfortable position for herself but she has done something to be sure that if I'm not fired, I will at least suffer in my new position. It takes all of my strength not to grab a paperweight and beat her painted face in.

I watch the boardroom door close on the secretary, the guest, and several of our more powerful members of staff. I feel a sense of foreboding bubbling from my gut and into my heart. I decide not to stay and work in the office.

This atmosphere does nothing for a creative mind and even less for one who has to focus on writing a page-three article.

I stop by the daycare and pick up my son. He excitedly tells me about how he got all of his words right today. I tell him that's great and that we will get him extra French fries as a reward. He has always loved words. I read to him every night and he says he wants to be a writer like me one day. I always tell him that I hope he is greater than me when he grows up.

After a quick lunch, I contemplate stopping at my sister's house to discuss the new development at work while the boys play. I feel a little unhinged inside; it's not often I have trouble holding myself together. No. Not today. I'm too tired to deal with her perfection or pity today. She'll just tell me I'm being a worrywart and that everything will be okay. Basically, she'll pat me on the back and be completely useless. I decide that we need a walk in the park to clear my head and burn off some of my son's energy.

The park is halfway between the town and my house. I couldn't have asked for a more perfect day and I am not the only one who has decided to take advantage of such a beautiful autumn afternoon. Lazy clouds drift across a perfect blue sky. Picnickers set up in the shade of the fruit trees. A few dogs wander and nose through the picnic baskets and coolers. Smiles are stretched across every face and laughter fills the air and melts with the melody from a guitar someone has brought along. All worries have disappeared. Neighborly disdain is temporarily forgotten. In this place, on this day, life is perfect.

I love the fall. The lush greenery becomes nature's canvas. She paints vibrantly with copper, golden, and scarlet tones. The stream at the base of the hill runs more cold and clear. The earth is damp and smells like new beginnings. Fallen leaves crunch underfoot and unseen animals can be heard making preparations for the coming winter.

There is a painter in front of an easel. She is facing the point where two of the violet hills meet. The first hill is brilliantly lit in the early afternoon light but casts a deep shadow over the second. Light and dark purples play off of each other in a complex pattern of natural splendor. The base of the hills is ablaze with vibrant autumn-colored trees. I watch the artist while my son is on the playset nearby. Such care is taken to mix pigments. Any wrong color could ruin the piece. The look on her face is of complete focus. When the canvas is on the easel, the rest of the world has vanished. Art- true art- is a world of its own. You must let it envelop and transport you to a place of beauty. When perfected this will give you the ability to transport others into your world. This requires precision. The colors must be right for people to truly see. Each brush stroke has a purpose. Each motion has meaning. Selection is key if people are to truly be transported to your world of serenity or turmoil. I miss being an artist.

I recognize her look of determination to convey herself. I see in her a reflection of me when I was in my prime as a writer. Each color is a word. I carefully covered my pages as she covers her canvases in beautiful art. But there is a difference. She is still creating something of beauty. I lost that gift. My muse is gone and I have nothing to show of my art but tattered remnants in second-hand bookstores.

I watch her for hours, almost forgetting to periodically glance at the playset to make sure my son hasn't been kidnapped. It would not be hard for someone to hide his little body somewhere amongst the sage violets. They were over two feet tall in some places and it would be easy to conceal such a tiny body. Eventually, my son tells me he is cold and wants to go home. I hold his hand, take one last glance at the canvas, and we head back to the car.

My brother-in-law is sitting on my front porch swing when I arrive home. Undoubtedly, he had not gone in for fear of having to hold a conversation with the wench. She doesn't treat him very well either. Upon seeing me pull into the driveway, he stands and smiles. He no longer has the carefully crafted muscles of a high school jock and his once long blonde hair is cut close to the scalp. He now has the happy belly of a well-fed husband but his eyes are still kind and his shoulders are still broad. I would be lying if I didn't admit that I've fantasized about an affair with him on lonely nights in my empty bed. It is only fantasy. He loves my sister and I could never do that to them. As much as

I sometimes want to kill my husband for choosing his mother over me, I can't cut him so deep either. My sister's husband has gorgeous green eyes that look right through me. It's hard not to fantasize that they show desire.

We were close when we were young. It's hard not to be in a small-town high school. He was in my grade and I had introduced him to my sister by accident when he came to my house for literature tutoring. I had had a little crush on him but their attraction was both instant and mutual. I would be lying if I said there wasn't a bit of jealousy on my part. Theirs proved to be a valuable match, however. Later, he attended the community college in the city and majored in criminal justice while my sister focused on her art at home.

When I would come home from the university on long weekends and holidays, he would beam with knowledge and explain the case studies he was learning about. He explained how different criminals tried to cover their tracks and what ultimately lead to their capture. He loved talking about the seemingly stupid little mistakes that people made like having pets and tracking fur to a crime scene or keeping their clothes that were covered in evidence. He was a wealth of information and, at the time, I had no idea how invaluable it would prove to be.

My husband and I had bought our house only two weeks after deciding not to pursue a life of travel. A friend of the family was selling and moving to the city, so she made us an offer we couldn't refuse. On the first night, I was feeling particularly forlorn. Everything I had planned for my life was veering off the road I had paved and heading straight into the river Styx.

I had stood in the kitchen window overlooking the hills. In the gentle moonlight, they had lost their purple luster and appeared to be several shades of black against a vibrant blue and wine-colored sky. The moon was bright and full and surrounded by three angelic halos. In the fog towards the valley, I saw my muse for the first time. The light from the resplendent moon had cast through the mist and produced a subtle arc of color. It was quite beautiful. I stared at it seemingly for several hours as I contemplated what was happening in my life. I was to be a mother. I was now rooted to these hills by a house that cannot move. My husband had gone for training and marooned me with the responsibility of tending to our new home by myself. What was happening to my life? How did everything go spiraling so far out of control? How dare this happen? What did I do to piss off Karma this much? The more I thought, the more my sadness mulled with anger.

I'm still not sure what time I had finally decided to try to sleep. I walked down a short hallway to a small bedroom. In the center was a mattress and box spring surrounded by cardboard boxes that awaited my family's help to unpack the next day. I had one last look out the window and saw a storm moving in. I pulled a blanket out of a box and cocooned myself as I cried into my mattress.

The next morning, it took a great deal of effort to roll off of that mattress. I didn't want to face the world, let alone my new life. Rousing myself was physically painful; I must have slept on my arm wrong. I dragged my feet to the kitchen where I dug the coffee maker out of a box. There was a can of coffee already on the counter. I had promised myself that, of all the things in my life that were changing, coffee would not be one (regardless of what the Nurse Midwife had warned about caffeine). As I listened to it brew, I rubbed my arm and noticed my shoes by the front door. I didn't remember leaving them there, nor did I remember how I had gotten them so muddy.

I had just leaned against the kitchen counter, deeply inhaled that rich aroma from my mug, and downed a dark, bitter, heavenly gulp when there was a knock on the door. Through the front window, I could see my parents, sister, and her soon-to-be husband. They were all bright-eyed and bushy-tailed and eager to help me unpack. I seriously wondered if the stork had been drunk when it delivered me to such a peppy family.

Everyone in the house was buzzing about the murder that had happened to the poor redheaded girl not too far away. She had been beaten to death by an unknown assailant with an unknown object. I listened to the details with a fascination that somewhat surprised me. My sister's future husband was shadowing the lead detective at the time and had information that hadn't been released yet. As I listened, I started to feel a tingle of inspiration. I pressed him further about how many bones were broken, where she had been attacked, and how the killer got in and out without leaving evidence.

That was it. My first of many books. I used this poor girl's death as my revelation and salvation. I ignored my despair at my new life and pocketed my anger at the world while I set to work. I spent weeks researching other killers who had beaten their victims. I interviewed the psychology professor at the community college and the lead detective on the case. My work was fiction, but her death would be the spark that ignited an inferno.

That was years ago. My muse hasn't been seen in quite some time.

I hug my brother-in-law. He is warm and smells like sweat and honey. He says he has been sent by the ball-and-chain (i.e., my sister) to borrow a muffin pan so she can make twice as many cupcakes at a time. I look at the back of my mother-in-law's head through the window. She is sitting in her chair with her back to the world, just like every day. She is toiling away at that awful blanket, pretending to ignore the world. I look at him and smile. I tell him I will bring it out to him.

I'm not sure if she senses my attraction to him or if it is just one of the bugs she likes to anger in my husband's ear. Whenever my brother-in-law comes to visit while my husband is away, she makes sure to tell him exactly how long we had been alone together and in what room of the house. Once, she had gotten him so riled up that he had questioned our son's paternity. That sent me into a rage that I didn't even know I had in me.

Today, however, I am choosing to make things easy for both of us. I go in, nod in her general direction, and retrieve the pan. There is no sense in making things more stressful than they already are.

When I return, he and my son are rolling a ball they had found back and forth across the wood planks of the porch. Those stunning green eyes look up at me. He comments that I look a little unglued. That's it. Something about genuine concern in those eyes becomes my breaking point. I crumble. Everything that I have spent the whole day repressing breaks out of me. In tears, I explain how much I miss being a writer. I explain that my friends and I at the paper will likely have a choice between losing our jobs or selling our souls to the fat algea that had come to work today. He holds my face in his massive and wonderfully firm pectoral muscles as I cry. When I finally calm, he releases me and tells me not to worry. I am just having a bit of writer's block; all of the great ones go through it. Once it clears, my job at the paper won't matter and my friends will all be okay.

I feign comfort for his sake. He pulls me in once more in a firm, loving embrace before releasing me and heading down the porch steps. I wave as he walks down the road. I turn and see the wench. She's now standing in the window with a smug look smeared across her wicked eyes. Her smile is pursed in the same manner as the Fashionista's had been this morning. I pick up my son and imagine myself wrapping the fabric strips in her hand around her throat and pulling tight.

This evening, I feel a little stir-crazy. I can tell my mother-in-law is plotting how to tell my husband about my brother-in-law's visit. She will tell him exactly what happened- without lying- but strategically word it so it doesn't seem like an innocent occurrence between family members. That's what we are. We are family. He is married to my sister. I envy the way they look at each other. Nothing less than undying love passes between them. I want someone to look at me with such devotion. I want to see myself in someone's eyes the way she sees herself in his. Poets spend their entire lives writing about that kind of love, but most don't truly know it.

Every day I love my husband. Some days I want to kill him. They say that's a sign of a good marriage. I have my doubts. So many days I just want him dead. Not just a simple heart attack. I want him to suffer. I want it to be something slow and meaningful. He, his mother, and his spawn have spent years draining life from me bit by bit; they have sucked my soul until I have become just an unoccupied exoskeleton of the butterfly I had been when we met.

I'm going to my dark place. I need to get out of here for a little while. I give my son some diphenhydramine and tuck him into bed. I don't even acknowledge the wench's existence as I pass her in her chair and head out the front door. The sun is setting. I look at the hills and think about a long walk. I decide against it. I feel like maybe returning to the park could ease my tension. Maybe the artist is still there and I can see her progress.

It is dark by the time I reach the park. The widely dispersed lamp posts provide very little illumination. I carefully select a bench in the shadows and watch. Darkness comes early in the fall. Though it is hardly past supper time, it feels oddly crowded in the dark. A pair of sweet young lovers walk their dog along the path. I can't hear the girl's laughter, but I can see it escape her by the light of the lamppost. Other couples collude on benches along the walkways. A gentleman in a hat leads two well-dressed ladies through a darker part of the park. Everyone has someone. Then there is me alone and cold on a park bench in the dark. I look up at the stars. Though they are bright and beautiful here, they disappear towards the city. Their natural beauty is engulfed by the light pollution emitted by the buildings below. I look down at the marker stone at my feet. "Bench dedicated in loving memory of Karen Philip." I don't know Karen Philip, but she is loved and someone is missing her. Will I be missed when I die?

I shake such thoughts from my head. I look back toward the eastern horizon. I can see the city rising up from the valley through the fog. It reminds me of a cemetery. Headstones of buildings mark the graves of the dead hopes and dreams of the people who work and live inside. I pray that is not my fate.

I walk along a paved bike path that connects the hills to the city by running through the small town. There's an old farm that no one inhabits, but still houses animals. The same Thoroughbred who was there when I was a child is standing near the fence. It is such a sad husk of an animal. A once beautiful mare has been left to rot. Skin stretches thin over the bones and open, oozing holes invite flies and feed their offspring. Her one remaining eye shows no life. Her will, her joy, and her soul are gone.

We stand in silent respect of each other's suffering before I continue to walk the path.

~ 9 ~

INTERSTICE

Getting out of bed every day is a struggle. It's becoming more of an act of The Gods than one of will. Some days I simply don't want to leave the comfort and safety of my bed. When I'm cocooned in my blanket, I am shielded from the world. It's warm, safe, and comfortable here. I don't have to entertain my son. I don't have to look at my empty computer screen. I don't have to face the wench. More often than not, getting out of bed is just too painful. Emotional pain is one thing but when it gets bad enough, it manifests as physical agony. My legs and arms don't want to respond to basic commands. They know what is coming if they move. When they do respond, they are rewarded with searing bolts of deep torture that results in spasms, locked muscles, and often crying. I'm so glad my husband doesn't see me like this. He's hardly ever home and when he is, he sleeps late into the morning and doesn't realize the struggle that is happening next to him.

On the days when The Gods are with me, I'm plagued by exhaustion. It doesn't matter how much I sleep; I do not rest. I get up and wander. I put my sneakers on and head to the hills. Upon my return, I lay back down. I lay awake in darkness and silence waiting for Hypnos to visit me. When I do finally sleep, I see visions of mutilated animals that I assume are my mind's metaphor for my life and career. I wake to the incessant buzzing of my alarm. I turn it off, fight through my pain, and rise to get my son ready for the day.

Today, The Gods are with me. Unfortunately. I rouse and stumble into the kitchen. The coffee is waiting for me. I love timers. I pour some into my favorite mug and hold it to my lips. The first inhalation of that aromatic heaven is just as important as actually drinking it. From the kitchen, I can see the wench in her chair. She's always sure to be awake before me so she can monitor my activity and report to my husband. I ignore her and start taking bowls, spoons, cereal, and milk out and placing them on the table. I hear her "humph" from the other room. She disapproves of my son eating cereal. As a wife and mother, I'm supposed to be up before the sun to make eggs, meat, toast, and fresh-squeezed juice for the whole family. Just one of the ways I am a failure as a human being who doesn't deserve her son.

I take my mug and head down the hall to my son. Our house is tiny and when my mother-in-law had set on moving in with us, we had hastily moved the nursery to the smallest bedroom which had been designated as my office. My office was now a converted storage space behind the garage. My husband had kindly put in a door so I could access it directly from the main part of the house, but I still felt a sense of bitterness at him for demoting me and our child in favor of his mother.

I set my mug on the gaudy primary-colored

nightstand. I sit on the edge of his little bed and look at him. I know I should be feeling a flood of emotion. I hear mothers talk of being overcome with feelings of love and affection that fill them when they watch their children sleep. They say their "heart could just burst" and there is an overwhelming urge to cry. I don't feel this. I am a mother. I love him. I care for him and I want the best for him. That is the extent of my emotion.

I rub his little belly and tell him it's time to wake up. His eyes open and he rubs them and yawns. He rolls over and lays his head in my lap. I pick up my coffee and drink with one hand while rubbing his back with the other. This is the most peaceful part of my day. I hear the shuffling of slippered feet down the hall and the wench peers in at us. I raise my mug in her general direction as she scoffs and continues toward the bathroom. I strain my ears to hear if she has slipped and cracked her head on the porcelain sink. No such luck.

I finish my coffee and wake my son the rest of the way. As he stumbles around (so much like his mother in the morning) looking for his clothes and waiting for the bathroom to be free, I head back to my kitchen for the next rejuvenating cup. I lean back against the counter and await my next drop of Ambrosia when I hear my cell phone from the other room. And now my day begins.

As with most mornings, I have my four a.m. text from my husband telling me to have a good day and reminding me that he will be home tomorrow. He knows I won't respond until I am well caffeinated but he still continues the daily ritual. We are not often in the same time zone so a "good morning" message could be at eight p.m. I do appreciate that he still does it. The other message is from my sister. She wants to harvest our late-summer crops and is asking me to join. Toil in the dirt with my sister or stay here with the Wicked Wench of the West?

I inform my son that he will be playing with his cousin today as I pour him a bowl of cereal. He gets excited and starts jabbering about which toys he wants to bring.

My sister's property is bigger than mine. Her husband keeps her and their family well cared for but my husband and I struggle. Some time ago, we decided to grow our own vegetables and raise a few chickens. She doesn't need to, but she likes feeling like she is contributing to the care of her family more than just raising their son and cleaning the house. It is also an excuse for me to come to visit more often. I don't like the latter reason, but it is a way for me to get out of the house and escape a few times a week.

I bundle up my son for the two-mile walk to my sister's house. Of course, we could drive there but, honestly, driving such a short distance seems so ridiculous. I never understood my coworkers at the paper who will get up extra early and jog six miles for their health and then get in a car and drive one mile to get a loaf of bread. These are the same people who complain about gas prices, traffic, and carbon emissions. Their logic is beyond me. Nature intended your daily life to be exercise and I intend to honor that and raise my son to do the same.

It is cold this morning. A fine mist covers the earth, causing the rising sun to bathe all of nature in a heavenly yellow glow. Ahead, I can see the old wooden bridge we had played on as children. It spans a cool, slow-running stream.

The nearly barren trees stand tall, guarding this paradise against outsiders. The water is calm. Not even the creatures beneath its surface dare to cause a ripple to disturb the tranquility.

Beyond the bridge, I can see the woods. They reach out over the water and call me to come near; to hide amongst their safe harbor. They beg me to speak my secrets, for they will never tell. I whisper that I will visit them later.

We continue down the road. My happy little lad is skipping and chattering. I know he is talking to me but it's amazing how little I hear. I don't mean to ignore him but they talk SO MUCH at his age...

My sister's house is quite a bit bigger than mine. Everything of my sister's is just a bit better than mine. There are, however, a few extra cars in her driveway. She has company. I'm never in the mood for company. We bypass the front door and head to the garden we set up half an acre away from the house. The chickens watch us closely. Filthy animals. They are lucky they earn their keep. We keep both meat and egg chickens in our flock. Good layers are allowed to live but those who do not prove their worth find a different value. My sister doesn't have the heart to kill anything and still buys her chicken at the grocery. She sees the birds as useful pets rather than supplies. I, on the other hand, have never found a problem with catching them or snapping their necks. Butchering them took some practice but it was never something I found psychologically difficult.

Behind the coop is our small grove of fruit trees. We have several varieties of apples (which provide more than we could possibly need this time of year), pears, crabapples, and a failed cherry tree. My sister had insisted on paying an obscene amount of money for nearly grown trees so we wouldn't have to wait long for them to fruit. I had told her it defeated the purpose of growing our own food to save money. She proved me wrong, however, when the trees paid for themselves and then some by providing enough fruit for her to make "Artisan Jams" to sell at the local market. We also have trellises of grapes, blackberries, and raspberries. Our husbands had built a heavy wooden fence around our vegetables. We had had a hard time with our first crops due to deer and other wildlife.

I don't mind feeding them corn or scraps, but this is for US and we had to do something to protect our food.

There are women here toiling in the garden. While my sister and a blonde I recognize from high school are up to the task and seem to be enjoying it, their friend doesn't even attempt to mask her disdain at the very idea of manual labor. Her heeled shoes and floral dress are entirely inappropriate for the day's activities. She clicks and pops her chewing gum as she leans against a post with a rake in her hand to keep her from falling over from boredom. A curious black cat watches from atop the slat wood fence in hopes that we might scare up a rodent or two for him. My sister knows how I feel about cats but he earns his keep too by eating the rodents and scaring the birds that eat at our produce.

The bored brunette looks relieved when she sees me. She grabs the blonde and says they don't want to overstay their welcome as she shoves her out through the wooden gate. My son sees his cousin digging in their "garden" in the corner- a patch of dirt that we periodically put plants in to make them believe they are growing things- and rushes to join him. I look at my sister with curiosity and inquire about the hasty departure of her friends.

She sighs and tells me that the blonde is reaching out for help. She is sure her husband is having an affair blah...blah...blah... I had been well apprised of this affair some time ago thanks to the gossip columnist at work. My sister reads the disinterest on my face and changes the subject. Her husband had told her of my outburst a few weeks ago and she asks if I am feeling better. I inform her that there is still no word. The stress is palpable and I skipped the last roundtable and worked from home to avoid it. She nods her head solemnly. She doesn't feel my pain. She hasn't "worked" in years. Her son and her home are a full-time job but she still manages to steal time for herself to paint or sculpt and she has sold quite a few of her works to supplement their household income. Is there anything she can't do?

We labor for most of the day. She offers me tips and tricks to jump-start my creativity. I appreciate her efforts but her art is very different from mine and she is a different sort of person. Her creative jumper cables won't work for someone like me. When it's time to leave, I take my buckets of produce up to the house to clean up before going home. On the way, my son selects a few juicy apples while I collect eggs. My sister says her mudroom door is blocked so we will need to go in the front.

The modest front door gives way to an over-the-top archway that pays homage to our British roots. Union Jack is adorned with faux gold flowers and renaissance style cherubs. The walls of her "grand hall" are a gallery of coats of arms. I'm not convinced we are related to any of them but she insists she did her research on our family history. So had I and there were a few skeletons in that closet (not to mention bats in that belfry). Every time I come in here, I'm reminded just how different we are. Cue the laughter sound bite. The kids are running down the hall ahead of us towards the bathroom to wash the mud from their hands. They are easy to track by the trail of muck and worms in their wake. I open my mouth to apologize but she just laughs. She says she needed to mop the floors anyway.

We take off our shoes and go to the mudroom to wash. My hands are caked in soil. My hair had long fallen out of the ponytail I had arrived in and clung to my back. I scrub at my fingers desperately but some stains just won't budge. On the contrary, her hands clean easily and her manicure is undisturbed. Her hair is still tucked tight in the bun it had been in this morning and though there was dirt on her face, her makeup was unsmudged. Is she magic? She worked just as hard as I did today.

She offers me a cup of tea before I hit the road. It's not coffee, but I'm not one to turn down caffeine in most forms. We sit at one side of the table and watch the boys in the living room. I hold the warm mug in my half-frozen fingers. We had worked so hard today that I forgot how cold I am. She smiles. She comments on how lucky we are. I tell her I agree though I feel a touch less lucky than her. Her husband will be home soon and they will have dinner as a family. They will then tuck in their son together and maybe read him a story. After that, they will curl up together on the couch and watch the television or talk to each other.

I, on the other hand, will go home and wash my vegetables. I will likely reheat some leftovers and serve my mother-in-law at the kitchen table while my son and I eat at the coffee table in front of the TV (another way I am a failure as a wife and mother) so that I don't have to be in her company. I will give my son a bath, we will read a story together, and I will tuck him in. I will then hide in the safety of my room or my office until she goes to bed. Maybe I'll get a little writing done, but I'm not feeling particularly inspired.

I thank my sister for a good day and the tea. I pick up my buckets of vegetables and bustle my son out the door. On the walk home, he chatters on about what a great day he had and all of the things he and his cousin hope to grow from the cereal, marshmallows, and other assorted "seeds" they had buried in the garden today. One day, I'll tell him what is happening in his little garden. Today is not that day. He is too happy.

We walk fast in the cold. The sun is already low behind the hills, leaving just enough light for us to see the way home. Our breath is silver in the failing light. My fingers are numb from the bitter air and the weight of the buckets of vegetables. My son tries to lift one of the buckets to ease my burden because he's a big boy and that means he's strong. I smile at his futile efforts and instead, ask him to CAREFULLY carry the little box of eggs from the top of the bucket. He beams with pride at such responsibility.

As we round the corner, I can see extra lights on in the house. Do we have company? Who would be over so close to supper time? We approach the door and I hear a familiar laugh. He's home early.

I take the eggs from my son before I open the door, knowing he will drop them upon the excitement of seeing his father. When the door swings open, he runs into waiting open arms.

There is my husband. His eyes and face are young. His stubbled chin could use a shave but his hair is neatly trimmed and carefully parted down the middle. When you look past his face, you see a weathered body. His shoulders are broad and through his tattered shirt, they are well-muscled. His cheek rests in a calloused laborer's hand as he listens to his son prattle excitedly. His arms are wrapped in rope-like veins that snake down his hands to his battered knuckles. The swelling in the joints of his fingers ensures that his wedding band- his most prized possession- can never come off. Though I may wish him dead sometimes, I do love this man and he loves me.

I come in and embrace him. It's not his usual "I missed you so much!" long hold. As we release, he gives me a sideways glance before averting my gaze. Something has upset him. I look at the wench. She appears sufficiently satisfied and I know she has spun my meltdown to my brother-in-law into something lurid. I will deal with that later.

I tell my son we must wash up for supper and he can help me peel the vegetables for his daddy's welcome home feast.

I clean some of our harvest and make a hearty vegetable stew with a large roast I have been saving for just such an occasion. With meat being expensive, we eat mostly the chickens and eggs that we raise for protein. As the stew and meat are cooking, I slice the apples we had selected earlier and sprinkle them with sugar and cinnamon before placing them in the oven. I turn and look into the living room. My son sits on the floor telling his daddy about the books we have been reading and about all of the things he has planted in the garden. Ignoring the wench, it almost feels like something on television. I, the mother, am in the kitchen while the father and son are on the floor in another room bonding. My husband had been gone for thirty-three days this time so I understand their need for time together but when did my life turn into this?

We all sit around the table as a family. My mother-in-law complains that I always overcook the vegetables and that one day she needs to teach me how to do it properly. I fight the urge to make a snarky remark in return. I don't like my son to hear our exchanges and she knows it. I intentionally overenthusiastically agree with her and tell her I think it would be good for her circulation to get out of her chair and her doctor did say that moving would be good for her arthritis. Cooking would be a great way for her to get moving! Okay, maybe a little snark does escape me. Her look turns sour. I smile.

My husband ignores the exchange and complements the roast. He meets my eyes and smiles for the first time all evening. My son, oblivious to the exchange between his grandmother and myself, says that his mommy is the best cook no matter what anyone says. My mother-in-law humphs. Checkmate. She will be satisfactorily bitter for the rest of the evening.

After a baked apple dessert, I wash, my son dries (mostly), and my husband puts the dishes away. Full-belly-induced yawning makes its rounds amongst us and we decide to continue the excitement tomorrow. My son brushes his teeth, changes into his pajamas, and comes into the living room with *Aesop's Fables*. We have been reading one every night. This typically takes some time. My son is younger than most beginning readers but it is by his own insistence that he not only learned to read early but also chooses stories that present a challenge for other young readers. In this regard, I see myself in him and I have chosen to nurture this passion.

We squeeze onto the tiny twin-sized bed with our boy between us holding the book.

After *The Crow and The Pitcher*, we discuss the moral of the story. I explain to my son that he could memorize a thousand books but, without the ability to think and figure things out for himself, it means nothing. My husband concurs and we kiss his head and tuck him in. I turn to our bedroom while my husband goes to say goodnight to his mother.

I bring the extra pillows out of the closet to put on the bed. My husband, having come from such a large family, had often slept in a pile of his siblings. Extra pillows make the bed feel less empty for him. It annoys me, having slept primarily alone until I met him (and mostly now), but little sacrifices make a relationship solid... right?

He enters and closes the door behind him. He picks up a pillow and starts to put a case on it. He asks me about the incident with my sister's husband. I remind him that I had told him about the stress at the paper and my heartache over my career. I assure him that it was nothing more than an available shoulder to cry on. He asks why I chose that shoulder. He knows of my prior crush on my brother-in-law, regardless of how long ago that had been. I bitterly remind him that *his* shoulder is never available. He grumbles about supporting the family but he understands. I tell him I don't know why he would let it ruin his day. We should be glad he is home, not fighting because his mother is stirring the pot again.

He states that he doesn't understand why we can't try harder to get along. I remind him that she has always hated me and our son no matter how hard I try. I also remind him of when his mother had called me a failure and told me I should give up my fantasies of being a writer. He had been sitting next to me at the time, stuffing his face with spaghetti. He didn't stand up for me. He didn't attempt to intervene. He just sat and ate as I attempted to defend myself. I had been in tears for days over that incident. Now, standing in our bedroom, he says he doesn't remember it ever happening and asks if he was even there. I stare at him in disbelief. He says even if it did happen, I need to just get over it.

It is in this moment when he states that he doesn't even remember one of the most gut-wrenching things that has ever been said to me, that I realize for as much as he loves me, he cares very little. I had convinced myself that it was hard for him to leave his son and me time and time again, but it just wasn't true. In the war between his mother and me, I will always be on the losing side. The pain I had felt when he hadn't stood up for me those years ago has now deepened. I'm speechless. I look at him, my mouth opens, but no words come out. I feel the backs of my eyes burning. I have reached a point so far past rage and sorrow, that my body simply cannot respond. I leave.

What else can I do? I feel... infuriated... devastated... disoriented... desponded; is there a word that combines all of these and multiplies that emotion tenfold? I understand the devotion of a son to his mother. I see it every time my boy brings me a flower or colors a picture just for me. But what about devotion to your wife? Is that commitment conditional? Does it mean less than what you have to your mother? I have given up everything for us and our family. My life, my happiness, my career, and my ambitions are all gone for you and for love and it means nothing.

I look around and realize that I am headed back to the woods near the bridge. I had promised earlier that I may return for a visit and in my blind emotion, I have kept my word. I know I can feel at peace in the safety of their branches. They are the outstretched arms of an old friend who wait to comfort me. This is where I belong. I don't want to be near him now. I don't want my son to see me crumble. Most of all, I don't want to see HER satisfaction in my current state. She had succeeded in what she had set out to do. She had driven that wedge so deep between us that the split could only worsen. There is almost nothing holding us together now.

My mind is whirling. I feel sick to my stomach; it is the only recognizable feeling I have. My arms are flailing and acting out my fury without my command. My voice is emanating a scream I didn't even know I could create. My knees are buckling and I fall to the cold earth. I don't feel anything. There are rocks beneath my hands and a cold wind blowing, but I feel none of it. The numbness of my frenzy has become corporeal. I can't hear the creek or the wind or the branches. My body and the world around me have become completely anesthetized.

I roll to my side amongst the rocks and mud. My head finds a flat stone as a pillow. I try to focus. I find my breath. I hear the wind. I taste the cold. I feel the stones. I am steadily coming back to the world. I lay here and focus. I must find myself.

Is this death? Is this heartbreak?

Epilogue

Life is a patchwork quilt. Each piece is a memory. Each color is an emotion. You don't know how they intertwine unless you follow the path along the seam. They are all connected stitch-by-stitch. Colors and patterns they would otherwise have no reason to fit together come together to make something beautiful- a rainbow of fabric.

For as long as I can remember, I have wanted to be a writer. I suppose it stems from my love of books. I would spend hours with my nose tucked in between pages. The ability to create beautiful new places and make people feel real emotions for characters that never existed was a magical power I longed to possess. This craft, however, cannot be forced. It is a nature that one must first be born with and then tap into.

From the time I could hold a crayon and sketch words, I tried to hone my skill. Great new ideas would fly into my mind and I would feverishly put them on paper, but they never looked right. The stories were good, but the magic wasn't there. I attempted writing classes but these were useless. I wanted to create more than mere artifice on paper. I wanted true alchemy of words. As an adult, I had achieved such sorcery.

When I wake, I am back in my bed. My head is throbbing and my vision is blurred. I lift my arm and find it covered in red. I see that the blood is soaked into the pillow and the sheets. I cautiously roll over and find my husband, cold and stiff. His throat is slit wide open. His eyes are wide and empty. I jump out of bed and rush to the wench's room. A knife protrudes from her chest and there is a look of terror on her face. I back away and turn sharply to my son's room. He slumbers peacefully and unharmed.

I rush to the kitchen and call the police. Who would do such a thing to my family? I was surprised at the calm in my voice as I explained what had happened to the dispatcher. She tells me not to touch anything and the police are on the way. She tries to keep me talking but I hang up the phone and look out the kitchen window at the early morning light. The sky is still mostly indigo with just a bit of orange on the horizon. There she is! My muse! It has been so long since I have seen her. I thought she had completely abandoned me. Yet here she is. My own family's death has brought her back. She is telling me I must write of the person who did this. I must tell her story.

I rush back to my office and begin to type. What kind of person would hurt a family? A jilted lover maybe? A jealous spouse? My mind is reeling with possibilities. I have not been so invigorated in years. There hasn't been a murder nearby since my last book. My family is dead. I should be devastated but I am not. They deserved this fate just like the vagrant on the corner by my house, the adulterous lovers the gossip columnist had told me about, and all the others. My family's death, just as theirs, would not be in vain, however. I would tell the world a variation of their story and they will live on. I look out my office window. She is still there. Iris has returned. She is my rainbow in mourning.

My name is Marie Joseph-Charles and I am a writer of love and death.

Why death? It is the undeniable fascination with murder and the macabre. What makes someone take the life of another? It's something many of us have pondered. It is easy to *say* I could never kill anyone but I have never been a mother protecting my child. I have never been held in captivity with only one way to escape nor am I a jilted lover. In writing, I can transform myself into any one of people and find out what motivates them and feel what it's like to take a life.

Why love? In truth, at my core, I am a hopeful romantic. Finding someone you want to wake up to in the morning and can't wait to tell about your day at night is a beautiful thing. That person who makes you feel whole is something so many of us long for. It is our nature to want this other half for ourselves.

I invite you all to join me in the exploration of those fundamental fascinations that are rooted in the human core: Love and Death.

www.ingramcontent.com/pod-product-compliance
Lightning Source LLC
Chambersburg PA
CBHW070732020526
44118CB00035B/1203